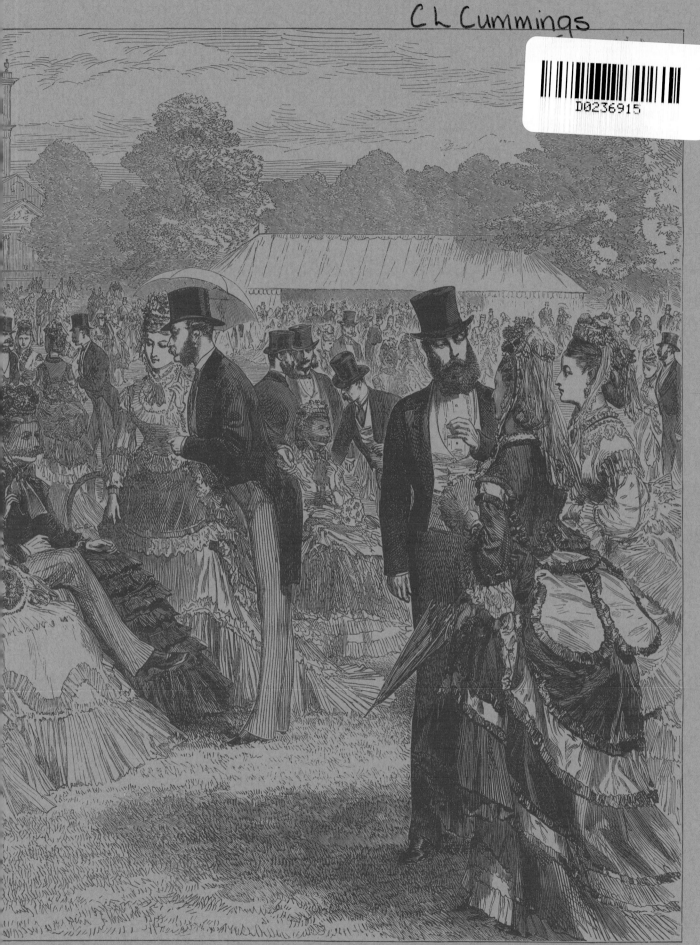

Buckingham Palace

The Prince Consort National Memorial, 1872.

The Salvation Army—A Service at the Head Quarters, Whitechapel Road.

HISTORY AS HOT NEWS
1865—1897

*The late Nineteenth Century world
as seen through the eyes of*
The Illustrated London News
and The Graphic

Compiled by
LEONARD DE VRIES
in collaboration with
ILONKA VAN AMSTEL

Foreword *by* Elizabeth Longford

Text abridged by
Ursula Robertshaw

JOHN MURRAY *Albemarle Street* LONDON

EDITORIAL NOTE

Throughout this volume the text is taken directly from the original issues of *The Illustrated London News* and *The Graphic*.

It has been difficult to reproduce some of the illustrations because most of the original blocks were destroyed during the First World War, and the original copies of the magazines are not always in good condition. Despite this difficulty, several of the illustrations have been included on account of their historic and dramatic interest.

Thanks are due to many for help and advice but in particular to Ursula Robertshaw for carrying out the necessary abridgements; to Ilford Ltd in connection with the illustrations; to the University Library of Amsterdam; but, above all, to the Editor and staff of *The Illustrated London News* for all their willing and invaluable co-operation.

Designed by Ilonka van Amstel
and printed in Great Britain by
Jarrold and Sons Limited, Norwich

0 7195 2848 8

FOREWORD

BY ELIZABETH LONGFORD

News in pictures. What recipe for pleasure could be so simple and yet so satisfying? This was the magical formula which carried *The Illustrated London News* to enduring fame and fortune. Founded in 1842, it pioneered a form of journalism which became immediately popular and has never ceased to proliferate. Now it notches up its 130th anniversary. Five years ago the first anthology of its selected texts and illustrations was published at 50 Albemarle Street, under the same historic imprint of John Murray which was in full vigour when *The Illustrated London News* was born.

The first volume, *Panorama 1842–1865*, brought us up to the end of the rich Victorian noonday. Its foreword was written by Sir Arthur Bryant. As one who owes so much to his learning, grace and friendship, I am enchanted to follow him in writing a foreword to *History as Hot News 1865–1897*. Sir Arthur has said that "to turn over the pages of the early volumes of *The Illustrated London News* was to experience a social revolution". The Britain of navvies, railroad workers and factory "hands" was inexorably ousting the gaitered farmers and smocked peasants. I cannot do better than say that, if the earlier story was one of social revolution, this second instalment is a grand repeat performance, with the social changes played in an ever higher, more insistent key. Moreover, it gains in scope and variety by including text and illustrations from *The Graphic* in addition to *The Illustrated London News* of which it was a follower.

There are two ways of reading great, panoramic journals like *The Illustrated London News* and *The Graphic*. The most usual perhaps is to float along with the stream, breathing in the atmosphere and forming an extensive picture of many continuous years—in this case thirty-two years (1865–1897), or the span of one whole generation. Sometimes one needs, however, to shut off the stream between lock-gates, so to speak, and study a particular portion of its course. It may be a battle, or a new fashion in ladies' hats, or Mr. Gladstone. In other words, one may read either for the flow or for the event. Students of the Victorian Age have always read *The Illustrated London News* for both.

Our opening year, 1865, was one of bland self-congratulation: "a moment of profound peace", as *The Illustrated London News* called it, "of unusual contentment, of singular prosperity". That characteristic note of Victorian optimism can almost always be heard in its pages, despite the trials to come. No doubt the very next year, 1866, was "awful", with war in Europe, panic in the City, commercial ruin everywhere. But only wait for 1867. A soaring year indeed, memorable for the Paris International Exhibition, followed two years later by the opening of the Suez Canal and the short route to India.

A certain blandness in fact pervades *The Illustrated London News* which must have suited that generation of Victorians. I say "blandness" not "smugness". No

newspaper has thrown more unforgettable splashes of black across its bright pages. Who can look at its portrait of the new ward for tramps in the Marylebone Workhouse without a salutary sinking of the heart? We are shown the cavernous building quite empty, its double row of coffin-like beds yawning to receive the first consignment of paupers. "God is Good" declares a painted rafter to any doubters below. It only needed a Frenchman, Gustave Doré, to draw the same ward in occupation, with the handsome Bible reader swanning down the central aisle, followed by the sardonic glances of his audience, to appreciate the peculiar tastelessness of later Victorian do-gooding.

The Salvation Army was at least free from humbug. It offered the same type of coffin-couches to its destitute women, but with the blunt wall-instruction, "Are You Ready To Die?" No wonder the vision of America flitted through so many dreams. We are shown the promised land through the eyes of emigrants, peering from their squalid ships at the dazzling Statue of Liberty—liberty and *life*.

One change, which has clearly come about in this mature Victorian world of 1865–1897, is a fabulous increase in sheer size. Vast shapes are for ever crawling up over the horizon, like dinosaurs of the manufacturing age. A monster induction coil, Krupp's giant gun, an enormous steam-roller for crushing stones. (In London's East End, stone-crushing was still performed as a special favour by pauperized clerks in top hats, wielding small hammers, for a wage of 9s. a week.) Certainly the massive chaos of horse-drawn London traffic seems even more violent than today. How did the indescribable mélée in Oxford Street ever sort itself out and get across the Circus? The team of brilliant artists assembled by *The Illustrated London News* and *The Graphic* saw many everyday operations almost as battelfields. Crossing the English Channel in the ferry looks worse than shipwreck. Shipwreck itself is a foretaste of Judgment Day. A house catches fire and burns like all Hell. A "demo" in Trafalgar Square stuffs the whole place from side to side and end to end with seething, bursting humanity. No Victorian dog ever stops bouncing and barking, and roving hordes of strays apparently cover the country. Only from the Royal Garden Party at Buckingham Palace do the milling crowds seem to be entirely absent and Society in total control. There was definitely more space then than there is today in front of the great marquee; nor were there any of those tremendous tight swarms humming round the Queen and Royal Family, such as twentieth-century custom has evolved. But outside this charmed circle, the nineteenth century ranted and roared.

Rather than despairing at this raucous, grimy, slummy London, *The Illustrated London News* is quick to detect and describe what it supposes are gleams of light. For the second year running it records that the marriage rate has fallen! Hopefully, it anticipates a smaller London population in the future, with no further demand for housing, except flats. Alas, London still cries out for houses nearly a century later; though the cleanliness and orderliness of the modern colossus would have taken our ancestors' breath away.

In many other ways times do not seem to have changed. In the 1870s, a dream of flying-machines. In our own 'seventies, a dream of space-living. Their "marvels of science" were Marconi and phonographs. Ours are video-tape and cassettes. The pictures of famine in India are painfully similar, over the years.

For outstanding events *The Illustrated London News* was unbeatable. No camera could have presented the incidents of the Franco-Prussian War and Paris Commune with greater feeling or variety. The woman shot for firing the Louvre is a minor Goya; Gambetta ballooning to safety, sheer joy. Splendid also are the great set pieces, such as the Suez Canal and the meet-ing of Stanley and Livingstone. Colonial conquest in Africa comes across resonant and ominous, with occasional vignettes which are both spine-chilling and funny, like the four white hunters being carried pick-a-back by four black servants through a mango swamp. How right that "our special artist" should have depicted the little old Queen on her Diamond Jubilee swept along to the shouts of coloured soldiers, recruited from all over the world.

Yet both the Empire and its artists had to go. The camera had to win. Just at the moment when engraving in *The Illustrated London News* and *The Graphic* had reached its proud zenith of speed and accuracy, the photographer superseded the wood-engraver. It had to come. News, it seems, must travel faster than fast and be hotter than hot. It is when the hot news of yesterday has cooled and become today's history that one can enjoy the best of both worlds.

CONTENTS

The dates refer to the issues of *The Illustrated London News* or *The Graphic* where identified

The jubilee of the Royal Conservatory of Music at Pesth, which took place on the 15th August, was celebrated with great éclat by the first performance of a new oratorio composed by the famous pianist Franz Liszt, who on this occasion left the seclusion of his monastic life at Rome, and reappeared once more in public as the conductor of the orchestra in executing his work. The title of this composition is "The Legend of St. Elizabeth". The story is told . . . by M. Otto Roquette, author of the libretto to which the music of Liszt is adapted. Her deeds of piety, with the miracles ascribed to her by the Roman Catholic legend, are set forth including the departure of her husband Ludwig to the Crusades; after which St. Elizabeth is cruelly persecuted by a wicked mother-in-law, who turns her out of house and home. Her death, and lastly, her funeral, are made the theme of some of the most pathetic and affecting music. The illustration we have engraved, from a sketch by M. Bartolomeus de Szekely, an Hungarian artist, shows the composer, dressed in the frock of his monastic order, in the act of wielding the conductor's baton on this occasion. It is stated that Liszt has undertaken also to produce a coronation hymn for the Emperor of Austria upon his investiture with the Hungarian crown.

[1865]

THE ATLANTIC TELEGRAPH EXPEDITION
(Illustration on next page)

The cable which, having been laid two thirds of the distance across the Atlantic, unfortunately was broken on August 2 last year [1865], since that date has lain two thousand fathoms deep at the bottom of the ocean. The diary of Mr. J. S. Deane, secretary of the Anglo-American Telegraph Company, has reached us, giving a detailed account of all the proceedings from July 27, when the Great Eastern arrived at Heart's Content Bay [Newfoundland], to Sept. 2, when the cable of 1865, having been secured, after three weeks' groping and grappling, by the combined efforts of the Great Eastern, the Albany, and the Medway, was attached to the finishing piece, about one third of the whole, which is now laid along the remainder of the distance to Newfoundland and in perfect working order.

[From the diary]: "What will Lieutenant Maury say to all this? For we hear that he has told the public that it is an impossibility to pick up the cable of 1865 . . . Where are the abstruse calculations about forces engaged in lifting the cable? Where are the theories about volcanic action . . . at the bottom of the Atlantic? What about the certainty of failure of gutta-percha as an insulator? Why, simply and practically this, the Atlantic Telegraph cable of 1865 has been picked up after a fortnight's hard work, and we are sending and receiving messages through it."

Testing the recovered Atlantic Telegraph Cable. (See preceding page.)

Meeting of the British Association at Birmingham Town Hall. Photography by the aid of Magnesium Light.

lions were, on Thursday [January 31, 1867], uncovered, in the presence of a large number of spectators, but without any formal ceremony. Lord John Manners, M.P., the First Commissioner of Works, Sir Edwin Landseer, Baron Marochetti, and other gentlemen walked round the square, inspected each lion, and expressed themselves satisfied with the work.   [1867]

ROMAN LONDON

An interesting addition has just been made to the evidences of Roman occupation by the discovery in the City of a tesselated pavement, in the course of excavating at the back of the Poultry for the formation of the new street from the Mansion House to Blackfriars. It lies about 17 ft. from the surface of the ground and though it is 1400 years old it is apparently fresh and perfect. It is of a bold type, of geometrical pattern. The tesserae are of five colours, by no means of brilliant hue; the outer portion being of common red and yellow brick, the whole laid in the ordinary Roman mortar, and upon tiles.

At last! Sixty-one years after the death, in her defence, of England's greatest hero; more than twenty years after the effigy of Nelson was, as it were, mast-headed on the top of the column in Trafalgar Square; and eight years and a half after Sir Edwin Landseer accepted the commission, the four lions designed to complete the Nelson monument have been erected in their places. The four

Roman Pavement found in the Poultry, near the Mansion House.

The locomotive crane at work on the Paris International Exhibition.

[Opened by the Emperor Napoleon III of France and Empress Eugénie on April 1, 1867. Demolished a year later.] Day by day the gigantic works in progress in the Champs de Mars show an evident advance of one step nearer towards completion. There cannot be less than a couple of thousand workmen employed within the building and about the grounds. Entering the latter through the gate opposite the Ecole Militaire we have what is styled the reserved horticultural garden, with its conservatories, pavilions, kiosques, lakes, rivulets, and waterfalls, and its marine and fresh water aquariums.

Many of the States are decorating the sections assigned to them in a most elaborate style. Portugal is dividing her courts with elegant Moorish-Gothic arches, Greece hers with rows of classic columns, and Russia hers with carved pillars and balustrades. Roumania is making a handsome effort to distinguish herself; the decorations in the Roumanian Court being exceedingly rich and elaborate—half Moorish, half Byzantine, as though intended to symbolise her present political condition.

In the English section of the park we observe a building in the domestic Elizabethan style of architecture, which looks very much like a national-school house; and in the rear of it are some long sheds, where models of munitions and implements of war fabricated in the arsenals and dockyards of Queen Victoria are to be exhibited.

At the extreme north end of the park the monster international club-house is in course of construction. Here members, strangers to Paris, are to be provided with everything they are likely to require, from an interpreter to a corn-cutter. This building will not only have its reception-hall, coffee, dining, smoking, reading, billiard, and bath rooms, but a telegraph and post office, and an arcade of shops, where every article that a visitor to the Exhibition can possibly want may be purchased.

ROYAL APPRECIATION
"The Queen is very anxious to express her deep sense of the touching sympathy of the whole nation on the occasion of the alarming illness of her dear son the Prince of Wales. [He had typhoid fever.] The universal feeling shown by her people during those painful, terrible days, and the sympathy evinced by them with herself and her beloved daughter, the Princess of Wales, as well as the general joy at the improvement in the Prince of Wales's health, have made a deep and lasting impression on her heart which can never be effaced. It was, indeed, nothing new to her, for the Queen had met with the same sympathy when, just ten years ago, a similar illness removed from her side the mainstay of her life, the best, wisest, and kindest of husbands. . . .

The Queen cannot conclude without expressing her hope that her faithful subjects will continue their prayers to God for the complete recovery of her dear son to health and strength.''

The Paris International Exhibition: The United States section, with American Planetarium.

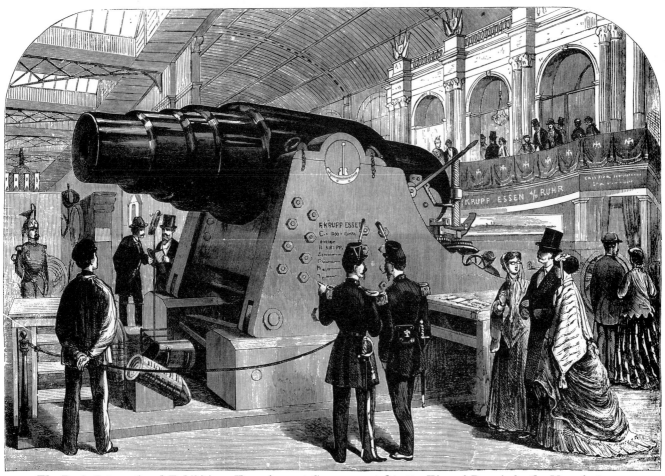

The Paris International Exhibition: Krupp's great Gun, presented to the King of Prussia by the Manufacturer.

[King Theodore II (1855–68) was the son of a small chief who, having organized himself an army by brigandage, was crowned king of Abyssinia in 1855. At first his rule was beneficent: he was advised by two Englishmen, J. T. Bell and W. C. Plowden, and his wife Tavavich was a good influence. But when Bell and Plowden were both murdered by tribesmen and his wife died, Theodore became unbalanced, quarrelled with the British government and imprisoned British subjects, including the British consul, C. D. Cameron. A British expedition under Sir Robert Napier defeated Theodore at Magdala, and the king committed suicide on April 13, 1868.]

January, 1868. The strength of the British army in Abyssinia is now becoming quite formidable. We have, in round numbers, about 6000 fighting men landed, and perhaps about the same number of followers, though it is not easy to determine, even approximately, how many followers of all kinds are distributed between Zulla and Senafe. Of muleteers there are, according to the last returns, 1365 for 4200 mules, and of camel-drivers 700 for 1739 camels. There are also 376 ponies, 257 draught bullocks, and 619 pack bullocks. General Sir Robert Napier has arrived, and taken the chief command.

March, 1868. Letters received from an officer at head-quarters state that Theodore has thirteen guns at Magdala, and that he is storing the place with provisions. He was also said to have intrenched his position on the Talanta plateau, where he had 10,000 disciplined troops, and was quite determined to fight. The British officers and men were anxious to storm the fortress.

On Good Friday, April 10, Sir Robert Napier sent the first division across the Bashilo, with the sole view of making a reconnaissance in force, having no intention of an immediate attack that day. Theodore's road on the south side of the Bashilo winds along a valley between the heights under Falla on the right, or west, and Islamgee on the left, or east; it winds up first to Falla Hill, and then, turning to the left, passes through Islamgee and Selassee to Magdala. Fearing that it might be dangerous to use this road any further, Sir Robert Napier directed that the reconnaissance should be made to the west of the road over the heights under Falla. However, Colonel Phayre, with a small party, pushed up this road, and, finding himself unmolested, he advanced

The Battle of Arogee, before Magdala, on Good Friday, April 10, 1868.

much further than was intended in the direction of the Arogee Pass, which opens on to a plain or terrace just under Falla, where Theodore was posted with the main body of his troops. As Colonel Phayre had sent off a despatch to say he had command of this pass, the artillery and baggage, with detachments for their protection, were sent along the road.

Theodore's troops, seeing only this small force, under Colonel Milward, and not knowing that that under Sir Charles Staveley was close at hand, and being moreover tempted by the sight of baggage to loot, could not be restrained from dashing down the slope of the Falla Hill. The onset of the Abyssinians was that of most barbarous nations. They rushed on with the bravery of ignorance. The Abyssinians held their ground for some time, even though Sniders, mountain guns, and rockets had begun to get fairly at them; but in the end the inevitable result of such a collision followed, and the enemy left 500 dead on the field, while not one man on our side was killed, and only nineteen wounded.

The *Times* correspondent writes:— "To describe the fight after the Snider came into play would be only to describe a battue. Its short cracks following each other in breathless succession were the death-knell of the Abyssinian cause. The unfortunate foe had no longer even the shadow of a chance, but went down like grass before the scythe . . . Sir Charles Staveley, as night was coming on and nothing more was to be gained by useless butchery, sounded the retreat. Theodore's famous guns gave the enemy no assistance whatever; on the contrary, they killed, it is said, a few of them. The big gun burst at the first explosion; the rest—there were about seven—kept up a steady cannonade but did not even touch one of our men."

The captives were released and sent to our camp on Saturday, the 11th, and on Easter Sunday, the 12th, while Theodore was endeavouring to obtain favourable terms. The *Daily News* correspondent reports: "At seven (in the morning of the 11th) a tremendous hurrah drew all loiterers first to the entrance of the camp, and then collected them in a group around Sir Robert's tent. Mr. Flad and Mr. Prideaux [British envoys] had come to us riding on Abyssinian steeds and escorted by two chiefs. Then for the first time we learned the completeness of the effect caused by our weapons. Two days before the action Theodore had butchered 318 native political prisoners, cutting the throats of and shooting some, and throwing about half down a precipice. His probable motives were partly fear, that they might escape in the confusion consequent upon our arrival, partly to impress us with a just sense of how terribly he could be in earnest when he chose. During the fight our prisoners suffered great anxiety . . . After nightfall the Abyssinian warriors returned, overwhelmed by the events of the day. At twelve Theodore admitted that he had been beaten, that the battle of the previous evening had ruined him; that half his army was gone, and all his bravest killed. In the afternoon came a letter addressed to the King of Abyssinia which, though couched in diplomatic phrase, demanded an unconditional surrender. Theodore wanted Sir Robert to enter some agreement, but Sir Robert would commit himself to nothing, and many

entertained great fears for his two envoys. Great, then was the delight of all when it was announced that in a few minutes all the captives would be in camp. About eight they arrived—a motley crew as far as dress was concerned—some in uniform some in old-fashioned and a few in Abyssinian costume."

The battle on Good Friday had cleared the way of the attack on Magdala, and by the discouragement it produced on the defenders made the capture comparatively bloodless. The description of the place makes it clear that without special good fortune the assault might have cost us a large number of our men . . . Had the army of Theodore remained in the place and defended it with the spirit it showed in the battle of the previous Friday, there must have been a heavy loss in forcing the steep, narrow pass leading up to a strong gateway. But before the actual siege came on the Emperor's force had become a rabble. Of the several thousand men who had obeyed his orders a few days before, only a few hundreds probably stood by him to the last. The end was that Magdala was taken with no loss on our side, and with but little on that of the enemy.

Magdala was destroyed on Easter Monday. The *Daily News* correspondent states: "The work of devastating Magdala—blowing up the gates, the magazine and burning the buildings—was entrusted to . . . the Royal Engineers. The sulphur and saltpetre in the magazine were scarcely more combustible than the houses themselves; everything burned like tinder, and the flames were rapidly spread by a steady breeze from the eastward. It was intended to have left the church standing as a testimony unto the heathen; but a pyramid of fire laid hold upon it and licked it up, leaving the church bell alone standing to proclaim by its silence the terrible fate of the tyrant who lies beneath those ruins, and who neither feared God nor regarded man. When twilight was beginning to spread over the hills, and the glow of the conflagration was brightest against the evening sky, the northern gateway was blown to fragments, and a last cheer proclaimed the work of mercy and vengeance fully accomplished. There was not in Magdala one living thing, nor one stone left upon another."

King Theodore having, upon the defeat of his army, abandoned his camp of Islamgee, and shut himself up in

The Destruction of Magdala.

15

the fortress of Magdala. After the storming, when the British troops forced their way into the fortress, his dead body was found, not near those of his chiefs in the gateway, but alone on the hill above. It is said that Theodore was fully conscious of the danger of attacking the British troops in the open field, and told his followers that they were no match for men who had better arms and better discipline; that they ought to act on the defensive from Magdala, or, if they were bent on attack, attack by night. This prudent counsel was overborne by the ignorant clamour of his warriors, eager for spoil and little used to defeat. After the fight they lost all their faith in Theodore's invincibility; and to his proud, imperious spirit, impatient of opposition and long accustomed to see himself feared and worshipped as a god, the last few hours of his life must have been intensely bitter. Twice his followers stood aloof from him, in sullen, resentful disobedience, when summoned to his side, and positively refused, when he invited them, as the last chance, to fly from Magdala, to accompany him and share his fortunes. At one time five of them even formed a conspiracy for seizing him and giving him up to the British;

King Theodore, as he lay dead at Magdala, April 13, 1868.

but at the last moment his marvellous personal ascendance reasserted itself, and their hearts failed them . . . On Easter Monday, Theodore and the chiefs retired within Magdala, and there awaited the advance of the British. As

the first soldiers appeared above the stockade the chiefs were shot down; but Theodore, who had already dropped his robe of Royal silk to escape observation, fled from the gateway to a retired spot higher up on the citadel, and there

The Naval Rocket Brigade firing rockets at Senafe.

16

shot himself, putting the pistol to his mouth.

In the instance of the war which has just been brought to so successful a conclusion there remain no regrets or self-reproaches which usually alloy the satisfaction of victory. Our object was in every sense a righteous one—to deliver from the hands of a semi-barbarous potentate those of our countrymen whom he had snatched from their peaceful or benevolent pursuits and laden with fetters; and, above all, to assert and vindicate the inviolability of the Queen's representative while engaged on her behalf in a

peaceful mission to obtain their release. Not until it was believed that all milder means had been exhausted were arms resorted to. A sense of national obligation was the sole impelling cause of this military expedition—not ambition, not greed, not glory. England desires only, with the rescued captives, to leave Abyssinia as nearly as possible as she found it.

Kassai, Prince or ruler of Tigré, reached Senafe on May 25, on a visit to Sir Robert Napier. A private interview took place on that day, and there was a public durbar next day, at which presents were given, and it was an-

nounced that about 800 muskets would be handed over to Kassai, and some guns and mortars. The next day Kassai was invited to come and see the performance of the Naval Rocket Brigade. Its armament consists of twelve rocket tubes; each tube can be carried upon a mule, with two boxes of ammunition. At Arogee these noisy missiles produced great consternation among Theodore's rash followers, and in the attack upon Magdala, on April 13, they were equally effective. The fame of the brigade had spread throughout Abyssinia, and the Kassai was most anxious to see these terrible instruments of destruction.

THE GREAT INDUCTION COIL

Many years have passed since Faraday announced his discovery of "induced electricity"; or of the fact that a galvanic current, when suffered to pass through a conducting wire, had power to engender another and distinct current in a second wire bearing certain definite relations to the former ... The discovery that very beautiful results were to be attained by passing the induced current through vacuum tubes has led to a large demand for induction coils as pleasing philosophical toys; and various makers have sought to increase their

power by increasing their size.

Professor Pepper has for some time been desirous to add a "monster coil" to the other attractions of the Polytechnic Institution; and, by the skill and perseverance of Mr. Apps, he has been able to attain his object. The great coil now exhibited is 9 ft. 10 in. in length and 2 ft. in diameter. Its core of soft iron is formed by a bundle of straight wires, each 5 ft. in length and ·0265 in. diameter. The diameter of the combined wires is 4 in., and the weight of the core is 123 lb. The primary coil

is of copper wire of the highest conductivity, and weighs 145 lb. The diameter of this wire is ·0925 of an inch, and its length is 3770 yards. It is wound round with cotton, and makes 6000 revolutions around the iron core. The secondary wire is 150 miles in length, and ·015 of an inch in diameter. It is covered with silk, and is wound into an outer coil 50 in. in length. The primary wire is insulated from the secondary by an ebonite tube $\frac{1}{2}$ in. in thickness, and the whole coil is enclosed in another ebonite tube and mounted upon substantial supports also covered with ebonite. The galvanic current for the

Queen Victoria opens Parliament: The Reception at the Peers' Entrance, February 5, 1867.

primary coil is furnished by a Bunsen's battery of forty cells.

When all was complete, it was found that the new coil would furnish a spark, or rather a flash of lightning, 29 in. in length, and apparently $\frac{3}{4}$ in., in width, striking the disk terminal with a stunning shock. The power of this flash may be estimated from the fact that it will perforate a mass of plate glass 5 in. in thickness.

To the visitors of the Polytechnic the new coil will be a source of endless delight and wonder. It was seen by their Royal Highnesses Princess Louisa and Princess Beatrice when they visited the institution a few days ago [April, 1869].

MR. CHARLES DICKENS'S LAST READING

[Dickens died on June 8, 1870; his readings are thought to have contributed to his death, especially the extremely emotional performances such as the death of Nancy in *Oliver Twist*.]

It is now fifteen years ago that Mr. Charles Dickens commenced reading his works in public, and received so much encouragement that he found it to his interest to continue the practice. Mr. Dickens was and is remarkably well qualified for the task. He possesses much histrionic power, and has more than once taken his part in stage performances, to the delight of his friends and many good judges. Last Tuesday

evening [March 15, 1870] Mr. Dickens brought his long series of readings to a close at St. James's Hall, choosing the Christmas Carol and the Trial from Pickwick. Those who have been accustomed to attend his readings will regret their termination. The author, too, cannot but have his regrets, very feelingly expressed in a speech with which he brought his ever-memorable farewell reading to a close, and which ended: ". . . I have thought it well at the full floodtide of your favour to retire from these garish lights I vanish now for evermore, with one heartfelt, grateful, respectful, and affectionate farewell."

POOR CHILDREN
OF EAST LONDON

The district church of St. John the Evangelist, in the poor and populous district of St. George's in the East, maintains several useful institutions for the benefit of the neighbourhood. The Ragged Schools, which were opened five years ago, Lord Shaftesbury being the president, have 310 children on the books, with an average daily attendance of 216, which tends to increase. There are likewise 120 Sunday scholars enrolled, with an average attendance of 40; and the attendance at the night schools averages 46. The Penny Savings Bank, the Lending Library, the Mothers' Meeting, and the Sewing Class, are instrumental also in doing much good. The soup kitchen, built at the expense of the committee, adjoining the schoolhouse, provides 1000 quarts of nutritious soup, during the winter, for distribution among the destitute and sickly poor; and a dinner dish of Irish stew is given, every Wednesday, to poor children attending these or any other schools on payment of one halfpenny each.

Mr. Charles Dickens's Farewell Reading.

Halfpenny Dinners for poor Children in East London.

19

WINTER IN BOSTON

(From our Special Correspondent.)

Despite the rudeness of the Boston winter, the young ladies are not in the least inclined to keep within doors. The English idea that Yankee girls are puny, listless, and indolent beings, is somewhat exaggerated. They have not, certainly, the general and ruddy health of their English sisters, and are not perhaps so devoted to those robust sports and lusty methods of exercise which make the daughters of Britain the finest physical examples of womanhood extant. Still the New England damsels are fond of out-of-door pastimes. In summer, go where you will, you will see at almost every turn, young ladies and gentlemen engaged in lively games of croquet—laughing and flirting, disputing good-humouredly on questions "of law or of fact;" that is, the rules of the game, and whether this ball hit that; in the mountains you will find the girls going upon long berrying or fishing expeditions; at the seaside you will see them rowing and bathing; and in the

Police Convoy in Boston.

Ladies' Window at the New York Post Office.

country you will not fail to note them mounted upon hay carts, going long jaunts through the woods on picnicking excursions, and roaming the fields in quest of wild flowers. Winter has its joys, not less cheery than those of the season of fruits and genial skies. When there has been a heavy fall of snow, the streets are straightway crowded with multitudes of sleighs. Some are light, airy vehicles; others are basket-like; yet others are substantial and elaborate, brass or silver-mounted, with painted panels, and filled in luxuriously with every variety of many-coloured skins and rugs. In this hearty, healthy pleasure of sleigh-riding, the ladies have their full share. The number and speed of the sleighs make street-crossing not a little dangerous; and our lusty policeman, with his sugar-loaf hat and fur gauntlets, finds a continual and, from the gallant expression of his face, we should say congenial employment, in acting as a convoy to the jaunty damsels who are anxious to get over to Thompson the jeweller's, across the street. The ladies are evidently dressed with ample provision for the inclemency of the season; and one notes with admiration that they have managed with great art to combine warmth with grace, and tastefulness of attire. Their veils are deftly wound about their throats, in such a way as at once to give an airy effect and to keep off the cold.

THE SEA MESSENGER

The little vessel represented in our Illustration has been invented by Mr. J. A. R. Vandenbergh of Portsmouth, to be freighted with letters and papers belonging to a ship in danger of foundering at sea, or in any danger of being wrecked. It will, in such a case, serve as the best vehicle for the preservation of records and important documents, and in all probability for their conveyance, by favouring winds and tides, to some near or distant shore. It is certainly much better than the ordinary glass bottle, which may be fractured by any floating spar or fragment of wreck; or may be dashed to pieces by the wave casting it upon a rocky coast. The water-tight and air-tight metallic hull of the "Sea Messenger", with its extreme buoyancy, will ride in safety through the most violent storms, and it has capacity to hold not only the ship's papers, records of the voyage, lists of the passengers and crew, and a brief report of the disaster, specifying the latitude and longitude and time of its occurrence, but letters from those on board to their friends, wills, or draughts of money, or bills of exchange, or any other papers affecting their private interests. Other uses of this contrivance will become obvious with its more frequent trial at sea.

The Sea-Messenger, to convey Letters from Ships in Peril.

THE PARIS SEWERS

Among the sights of Paris, which provincials and foreigners are most anxious to see, are the gigantic collecting-sewers beneath the city. The main artery of these extensive subways on the northern bank of the river is between three and four miles in length, and extends from the Place de la Concorde to Asnières. It is only on certain days of the year that the Paris sewers are made show-places of. On these occasions they are magnificently lighted up with some thousands of moderator lamps ... The boat is provided with a movable crescent-shaped fan, pierced with holes to admit of the water flowing through, which, on being let down, fits exactly to the rounded bottom of the sewer and pushes before it all the solid refuse matter that may have accumulated. The boat is capable of holding some fourteen or sixteen people.

A Trip round the Sewers of Paris.

Of the many public works and improvements projected and carried out in Egypt under the auspices of the present Viceroy, Ismail Pacha, the dry dock at Suez may fairly take rank as first in importance and utility. Hitherto the navigation of the Red Sea has been impeded for want of dock accommodation at Suez. Vessels requiring cleaning or extensive repairs have up to the present time been sent to Bombay, a voyage of fourteen or sixteen days; or,

if the emergency was great, or repairs of only a trifling nature were required, the vessels were beached at some distance from Suez—a proceeding involving much risk, which captains did not care to incur.

The dock is constructed upon the end of a spit three miles from the town of Suez, and within a mile of the anchorage in the roads. There is deep water at the entrance, and in connection with it a fine port is in course of construction.

The following are the dimensions of the dock: Length inside, 413 ft.; breadth at the top, 95 ft.; breadth at the bottom, 74 ft.; depth at high water, 39 ft.; depth at low water, 24 ft. The time occupied in filling the dock, including the working of the caisson and putting the ship in the basin, is two hours and a quarter; and the time required to pump out the water without a ship in the dock is six hours. It is hoped to have one of the jetties ready in four months' time.

Opening the New Dry Dock at Suez.

M. FERDINAND DE LESSEPS

M. de Lesseps is one of those great men of practical invention and administrative execution whose genius, directed in the present age to objects of public utility or to commercial and industrial undertakings, has achieved a truer glory, by serving the common welfare, than that of the most Napoleonic victories in war. It was he who suggested to the late Said Pacha, being on terms of confidential intimacy with that gentleman, the scheme for a maritime canal between the two seas; and the

Compagnie Universelle de Suez was accordingly formed in 1854. It is now on the point of completing the great mechanical task of construction under the direction of M. de Lesseps.

THE MARITIME CANAL

The Maritime Canal is to extend from the newly-constructed artificial harbour of Port Said, on the Pelisian coast of the Mediterranean, to the port of Suez, at the head of the Red Sea. The length of the canal is not quite a hundred miles. Its depth throughout is to be 26 ft.; its

general width is to be 246 ft. at the base and 328 ft. at the top of the banks, except in some portions of the line, where it has to be cut through high ground; the width here is reduced to 190 ft. at the upper part. There will be no locks on the Maritime Canal. Vessels will be able to steam through, or be towed through, from sea to sea in about sixteen hours. The Compagnie Universelle du Canal Maritime de Suez was formed in 1854. The canal, with its ports at each end, when finished, was to be the property of the Compagnie for ninety-nine years, after which it would belong to the Egyptian Government. Meantime, that Government was to receive annually 15 per cent of the traffic earnings. These conditions are still in force.

The wages of the workpeople employed on the canal are by piece-work, averaging 1s. 6d. or 2s. a day, the company finding tools.

Opening of the Suez Canal: The Procession of Ships in the Canal.

OPENING OF THE SUEZ CANAL

The imposing ceremonies and international festivities at the formal opening of the Suez Maritime Canal on Tuesday, Nov. 16 [1869] were honoured with the presence of the Empress of the French, the Emperor of Austria, the Crown Prince of Prussia, and other Royal persons whom the Viceroy of Egypt had invited. On November 17, a procession of some fifty vessels, including the steam-yachts of the Empress of the French, the Emperor of Austria, and the Viceroy, with a Prussian frigate, a Russian vessel of war, various passenger steam-boats, pleasure-yachts, and merchant ships, went through the northern half of the Canal, from Port Said to Ismalia . . . The largest vessel that passed on this occasion all the way from Port Said to Suez was the Egyptian Government steamer *Peluse*, drawing 16 ft. of water and 250 ft. in length; but Commander Nares, R.N., of the British Admiralty, who took soundings all the way, states in his official report that vessels drawing 17 ft. could pass through with ease. He states that, except for about ten miles, there is a depth of 24 ft. throughout the entire length of the Canal. The grounding of several ships, on the November 17, was caused by their own over-haste and blunders, not by any fault of the Canal.

It is impossible not to contemplate this magnificent achievement without emotion. Not only does it excite our sense of admiration, but it suggests thoughts and stirs feelings, and awakens hopes, all of which carry us into the far future, and connect themselves with the progressive development of the human race. Here is a work which may tell with beneficent power upon the conditions of nations, East and West, for ages yet to come. To some extent we may estimate the direct material advantages which will accrue from the opening of a short channel of water communication between the Mediterranean and the Red Sea—or, speaking on a wider view of the case, between the Atlantic and the Indian and Pacific oceans. But who can pretend to foresee the vast variety of moral influences which will take their origin from this apparently slight geographical change; in what manner they will act and react upon nations even the most remote from each other; what will be their effect upon social customs, modes of thought, and habits of life; or in what degree or with what results they will modify the philosophies or the religious beliefs of men coming fully within their range? Happily, the glimpse we obtain of the likelihoods and possibilities harmonises with the confidence we place in the laws which govern human destinies, and encourages us to anticipate from it a vast preponderance of good over evil.   [1869]

The Isthmus of Suez Maritime Canal: Bird's Eye View of Entrance to t

...nal from the Red Sea, with New Harbour, Docks, and Town of Suez.

THE FRANCO-PRUSSIAN WAR

Parisians consulting a Map of the War.

[Following the victories by Prussia over the Austrians and their German allies in 1866, the French re-armed and Napoleon III tried unsuccessfully to form an alliance with Austria and Italy. War with Prussia was declared on July 20, 1870, the ostensible reason being the dispute over the candidature for the vacant Spanish throne. The armistice was signed on January 28, 1871 after a crushing military defeat of the French. The Prussians lost 28,000 dead and 101,000 wounded, the French 156,000 dead and 143,000 wounded.]

Paris, July 21, 1870. So far as Paris is concerned, the war may be said to be popular. Every evening the circulation of carriages is impeded by a procession of vehicles decorated with coloured Chinese lanterns, and conveying men bearing flags and sounding those immense *cors de chasse* with which French sportsmen are in the habit of intwining their bodies. Walking at the sides and following in the rear are crowds of men in blouses singing "The Marseillaise", or the equally popular "Mourir pour la Patrie," while the stream of loungers on the foot pavement of the Boulevards are every now and then swept aside by parties of young men with arms linked together or waving their sticks over their heads and shouting "Marchons! Marchons!" at the top of their voices.

Paris, December 10, 1870, twelfth week of the siege. With reference to the all-important subject of provisions, I may note that fresh meat has now become extremely rare, and that the only kind regularly rationed out is horse-flesh; while, as regards the salt meat, this is simply detestable; and as for the dried haddocks, they are incredibly nasty. No wonder, therefore, that the gourmets who commenced eating dogs, cats, and rats, by way of diversion, should continue feasting on this more palatable though unclean food.

Defence of Paris—Battle of Villejuif.

THE BOMBARDMENT OF SEDAN AND STAMPEDE OF THE FRENCH SOLDIERY

The sketch is from M. Mejanel's pencil, who was in the thick of the bloody business. Remaining on the high ground, as long as it was safe to stay, he was able to perceive clearly how the Prussians were gradually converging on the fated stronghold. It is probable that in this instance, as in many others during the present war, the French were outmanoeuvred for want of sufficient information of the enemy's movements, and, being outmanoeuvred, were presently outnumbered.

Early in the day, according to a statement of a French officer, everything seemed to bode well for the French cause, and Marshal MacMahon was assured of victory. But, presently, two sinister omens of the battle occurred. MacMahon was severely wounded, and a strong body of Prus-

sians appeared on the left of the French forces. Swiftly, yet methodically, the German Artillery approached the French lines, and hemmed them round with a circle of fire. Their aim was wonderfully precise. Already the French had begun to waver. Numbers of stragglers were seen quitting the lines of fire, and when the Emperor re-entered the town by the Balan Gate, amid a storm of projectiles, during which several of his suite were struck down, he found the streets filled with disbanded infantry who had deserted their colours, and were crying out for cartridges. And now the bombardment became truly terrible. Sedan is built in a hollow, commanded by heights about a mile distant. The Prussian Artillery directed a plunging fire into the town, and threw shells among the

helpless throngs of human beings who crowded the streets. Routed combatants, townspeople and peasants who, for security, had sought the treacherous shelter of the city, were all included in one common massacre. The ramparts were, it seems, unarmed, while the cannon of the citadel consisted only of four 24-pounders. Ammunition and food were both failing, an attempt to break through the enemy's lines would have been hopeless, and so, at a council of war held at the Prefecture, it was resolved to avoid further slaughter by capitulation.

We have probably, as yet, not heard half of the tragic occurrences of that terrible First of September, but we know enough to comprehend the dreadful sufferings to which the inhabitants of fortified towns become liable in time

A Captive Balloon at Montmartre.

the most advanced post of the Prussians army before Metz; and he writes the following account of it: "We saw a number of people coming from Metz who were civilians desirous of getting away from the beleaguered fortress and from the distress which all can understand must be the fate of those left within it. The group who came along the road consisted of men, women, and children, all carrying bundles; and a woman came on in advance with a pocket-handkerchief on a stick as a flag of truce. But the Prussians, who had determined that they would not allow any more of the citizens to leave the city, and had notified those in command that all parties attempting to escape would be fired upon, now kept their word, and the pickets around us began, as the group approached, to fire upon them. We could clearly see the party as they came up the road. One man, who made himself unfortunately too conspicuous, was observed to fall. The group wavered; the foremost figure, with the white flag, still advanced; but at last she looked round and perceived that all her companions were flying; upon which she understood her situation and followed them back."

[October 15, 1870] The last few days have had their full share of those of war. It would seem, as a rule, to be safer to stay in the open country, where, under the firm discipline of the German armies, forced requisitions are the worst penalty to be encountered, than to seek the false security of a fortress. The experience of this war has proved that fortresses are invaluable as centres of defence and rallying-points; but it is evident that they should be dissociated, as much as possible, from non-combatant existence. Even when soldiers merely contend with soldiers, war is bad enough; but when helpless women and children are slaughtered just because they cannot avoid the bullets, war becomes fiendish.

[Marshal Bazaine and the fortress of Metz capitulated to the Prussians on October 27, 1871, with 150,000 prisoners, including 20,000 sick and wounded.]

The scene witnessed and depicted by our artist took place at Mercy le-Haut,

Siege of Metz: Inhabitants trying to leave the City before its Surrender.

The Storming of Bicetre on the Outskirts of Paris by the Bavarians.

bizarre and novel incidents which have characterised the later stages of the war. Paris, though closely invested, can still communicate with the outer world. The service of the *poste aero-statique* is conducted with some pretence at regularity, and the escape of M. Gambetta from Paris was effected by the same agency. In company with another balloon the car in which the minister took his seat sailed gaily over the Prussian lines amidst a storm of shells and rifle bullets, one of which even grazed the arm of the distinguished voyager. Adverse currents drove him in dangerous proximity to the hostile encampment before Metz. At length, however, he was enabled to descend near Amiens. . . .

In Paris every voice is still for war. The German siege guns have not yet opened fire, though their batteries already crown the heights behind Sèvres, St. Cloud, and Bougival. A new shell is to be employed on this occasion, manufactured by the famous Krupp; it is to be in the shape of a bolt three feet in length. The charge of powder weighs 70 lbs. and just fills up one foot of the interior. Trochu [Governor of Paris] and Rochefort have done wonders in a short time, and Paris is now absolutely impregnable, against assault or surprise. The bombardment it is expected will be directed in the first place against the forts.

For the moment, however, the food question is uppermost in the minds of the inhabitants. Meat is already getting scarce, and nondescript scraps of dubious origin are set before guests at restaurants formerly of high repute.

The great herd of oxen which were seen a few weeks ago in every open space have not been all consumed; they have been salted and stowed away against the evil day. Of wine there is even an abundant supply; and bread, unless the Prussian shells destroy some of the great corn stores, will not be wanting for long months. But there must soon be great distress in the city, as there is now among the poor. Already 300 of our own country people, who, from poverty or failure of remittances, were unable to leave Paris in time, are being fed from a daily soup-kitchen at the Embassy. Unless the garrison can compel the enemy to raise the siege, or the provinces fall on him in the rear, the fall of Paris, like that of Strasbourg, is simply reduced to a matter of arithmetical calculation.

Transporting Wounded by River Steamers, on the Canal de la Marne, to the Paris Ambulances.

Killing an Elephant for Food in the Jardin des Plantes, Paris.

Paris, January 1, 1871, sixteenth week of the siege.

Diverse expedients have lately been adopted in Paris for carrying on the defence of that unfortunate city. Eating is quite as important a part of this business as fighting, and the approach of hunger is more to be feared than a Prussian bombardment or assault. It was found advisable to order the killing of the wild beasts in the zoological collections, both at the Jardin des Plantes and at the Jardin d'Acclimatation, as well to save the fodder, corn, hay, and horseflesh which they had been accustomed to consume, as to make the flesh of such animals as the human appetite can stomach available for the public need. The deer, the antelopes, the kangaroos, the bears, and even some portions of the largest graminivorous beasts, such as the elephant and rhinoceros, would afford tolerable meat. They were quickly put to death by shooting, and their carcasses were sold to the leading restaurants in the city....

The worst hours of the bombardment are still to come, and though Trochu, who has already held out for four months, may struggle on to the end of the fifth, the last weeks of the siege will in that case witness the sorest trials of all, with hardly a gleam of hope to save the city from despair.

March 18, 1871. Parts of Paris, comprising the Champs Elysées and the Place de la Concorde, were occupied by 30,000 German troops from the Wednesday morning to the Friday morning of the week before last. . . . The spacious road was filled with commissariat waggons loaded with provisions for the army of occupation, and with provender for its cavalry. German troopers had taken off their knapsacks, piled arms, exchanged their pointed helmets for caps, and were cooking their dinners amongst the withered remains of exotic shrubs. Up the side streets might be seen soldiers on foot and on horseback looking for their lodgings with the deliberation peculiar to the Germans. Others were preparing, when night came, to bivouac in the open air. On the benches by the side of the road were seated some of the invaders, in groups of twos and threes, chatting and smoking their pipes, and ready to chaff any Frenchman or woman who might be willing to converse. Soon they became centres of animated crowds; and whenever one saw forty or fifty crammed together in a circle, one might be sure that Hans or Fritz was the centre of it.

An Object of Great Curiosity.

The Paris Boulevards during the Siege. Sketch by Balloon Post.

A MEETING OF A RED REPUBLICAN CLUB

The Paris clubs, which since 1789 have always had a revolutionary tendency, have been the cause of much of the ill-feeling and discontent with which the Paris populace seem to be so thoroughly imbued. During the siege the most bitter invectives were launched against the Government by the various Radical orators who would hold forth at these meetings; since the evacuation the vehemence of these assemblies has increased, and, at the moment we write, the Jacobin Clubs rule Paris. The Radicals are lauded to the skies; while their more Conservative opponents are declared to be traitors and only fit for the guillotine. . . .

CIVIL WAR IN PARIS

March 15, 1871. When we wrote a short time ago, that the departure of the Germans from the neighbourhood of Paris would probably be the signal for revolutionary demonstrations, we willingly admit that we did not anticipate a complete and disgraceful overthrow of order and authority. We did believe that the dangerous classes would seize the occasion, that they might be assisted by the artisans who could not obtain employment, and that aid would also be afforded to them by those who have so long enjoyed the playing at soldiers and swaggering about, while taking money on pretence of service which they were afraid to render . . . But we own that the shameful scenes which have been enacted in Paris, and which are still proceeding, have come upon us with a painful surprise.

The Mob is master of Paris. The Government has fled to Versailles. Numbers of the National Guard have become rebels, and numbers of the regular troops have become traitors . . .

Taking down the Red Flag from the Grand Opera House, Paris.

The Hotel de Ville, the Place Vendôme, and all the other points, the possession of which means the control of the capital, are in the hands of the revolters.

Barricades are thrown up in all important quarters and are manned by the ruffianism of the metropolis. Socialism again asserts itself in an edict against the payment of debts, and another which deprives the owners of houses of the right of ejecting lodgers. The features of the first revolution are being reproduced with a startling fidelity of imitation.

April 1, 1871. The Reds hold Paris, their organ preaches assassination, and the National Assembly votes that the case is not one of urgency. M. Thiers and his colleagues have permitted the rebels to elect the Commune, whose sign is the red flag, and whose creed is murder and rapine. . . .

April 15, 1871. Correspondents differ strangely in their accounts of the state of Paris, and while some tell us that no man's life or liberty is safe, and that it is a terrible thing to be under the sway of a secret tribunal of tyrants, others avow that things are by no means so disagreeable, and that if men keep quiet there

Encounter between the Revolted National Guards and a Company of Chasseurs in the Place Pigalle, April 18, 1871.

is no particular danger. It is certain, however, that arrests are constantly made, and that to be accused of what will speedily be called, as in the old revolution, "incivism", is to be sent to prison.

May 27, 1871. M. Thiers permitted the army to enter Paris on Sunday last, and in a few hours a large part of the city was in the hands of the Government and 80,000 soldiers were inside the walls. But gangs of revengeful savages, flying before the soldiers of order, fired Paris. The Palace of the Tuileries is a blackened shell. The Louvre was in flames, but there is hope that it has been partially saved. As yet we wait for details of the extent of the crime committed by the Commune, the crime in which those who could have stamped out the revolution at its outbreak, and those who could have driven it from the city upon the bayonets of Versailles, are more or less accomplices.

(*Left*) *Last Stand of the Insurgents at the Barricades.*

A Woman shot for spreading Petroleum.

The smouldering Ruins of the Hotel de Ville, Paris, burned by the Insurgents.

THE LAST DAYS OF THE COMMUNE

Terrible scenes have occurred in the final conflict between the insurgents of the Red Republican faction and the troops of the regular army, serving the Government of the National Assembly at Versailles. The fighting at the street barricades, renewed day after day, from one end of Paris to the other; the burning of several palaces, Government offices, theatres, and other public buildings; the shooting of some hundreds of prisoners, taken in the act of murder or of arson; and the removal of many thousands more, destined, probably, to a long penal transportation, are the chief incidents of the last days of the Commune. They are the effects of

The Burning of the Tuiler

ris, May 1871.

what Tennyson, in his "In Memoriam," has called "the red fool-fury of the Seine"; of that spirit of mingled vanity and bitter fanaticism which is ever ready to sacrifice law, justice, charity, and humanity, the safety and honour of the country, all prudence, decency, and commonsense, to the gratification of party ambition or party spite. . . .

The streets of Paris were slowly but surely occupied by the regular troops. To mount the houses was easy enough, though the doors often had to be broken in; presently the muzzles of rifles were poked through the upper panes, and sharp cracks and thick puffs of smoke coming out showed that the men had settled down to their work. The barricade was a more difficult matter, as it had to be made in front of the enemy's fire; but it was contrived with wonderful coolness and rapidity, the civilians who stood by eagerly bringing stones. Two or three barrels appeared to aid the construction. By pushing this barricade cautiously across the street, lying down under cover of one bit as they built another, the soldiers soon had cover enough to fire, comparatively at ease, straight up at the insurgents' barricade, while their comrades at the windows

took it from above in flank. As soon as a barricade was captured, the red flag was taken down and the tricolour flag was put up instead. The defenders of the barricade sometimes yielded themselves prisoners; in other cases they refused quarter and persisted in firing on the troops; or they rushed to a last hand-to-hand combat, with savage cries of "A la Mort!" Upon these occasions not a man or woman escaped the death they sought.

PARIS FASHIONS FOR 1872

Parisian fashion, discreetly enough, still continues to confine itself within modest limits, spite of the efforts which are every now and then being made to bring about a return to the extravagant toilettes of the Second Empire. Costumes de promenade are alike sober in colour and simple as regards trimming; woollen materials, moreover, in lieu of velvet, being principally in vogue, and the favourite shades being deep naval blue, warmish brown, myrtle green, violet, and a peculiar bronze tint that has lately come into favour rather than more brilliant colours. The trimming consists of braided arabesques or narrow

bands of velvet of the same shade as the material, and silk fringe. Chinchilla and ermine, the latter of which has been greatly neglected of late years, appear to be the mode during the present season, astrakan being reserved for the trimming of cloth polonaises, which form tunics and corsages at the same time.

Chapeaux are small, and of rounded shape, their turned up fronts reminding one of visors. Curtains [veils] are still wanting, but promise to make their appearance before long. Coiffures have undergone considerable change. The hair is thrown up in front in the Louis XIV and XV style, while behind it hangs like a loose chignon in a thick net.

NEW STREET TRAMWAYS

Last Tuesday week [May 3, 1870] the first London line of the Metropolitan Street Tramway Company, running from Brixton to Kennington Park, was opened to the public; and on Monday [May 10] a second line was inaugurated at Mile End.

The question has often been asked why London, like Berlin and Vienna,

The Brixton and Kennington Tramway, Interior of a Carriage.

should not have a regular network of tramways; but the difficulty of keeping a line of rails sufficiently clear in a crowded thoroughfare has hitherto deterred speculators from attempting to establish such a system. Now, however, new and vigorous attempts are being made to bring forward this really excellent mode of locomotion. The Kennington and Brixton line is a fair specimen of these tramways. The rails, which have deeper grooves than those at Vienna, thus rendering the car much less liable to be thrown off the line, are bolted on sleepers placed lengthways, and not crossways as on an ordinary railroad. The car is a handsome and commodious vehicle. It will hold twenty-four inside and twenty-two out, without causing the slightest inconvenience or crowding to the passengers. The car is drawn by two horses at a pace of about seven or eight miles an hour, and can be stopped in its own length. The brake used is most powerful, and brakes all four wheels at once. The fare for the journey is 2d, paid on entering.

THOMSON'S ROAD STEAMERS

The adaptation of the locomotive to common roads has long been the object of numerous and varied experiments. A machine has recently been constructed which has every probability of soon becoming a common traveller on our high roads.

The great peculiarity in this road-steamer is, that the wheels are bound round to the depth of five inches with an India-rubber tire. This covering, which does not at first sight appear capable of sustaining much hard work possesses innumerable advantages, being at the same time perfectly noiseless, and exceedingly durable. It also enables the steamer to pass over wet grass and newly made land with an incredible ease and lightness—an immense improvement on the ponderous traction engines which, a few years since, were wont to wander round London, to the intense disgust of coachmen, and to the terror of nervous invalids, and which, even now, cause great apprehension by their midnight prowlings about the country roads.

The steamer is commonly used to draw an omnibus or carriage. It is also, however, capable of dragging a plough, thus successfully solving the problem of ploughing by direct steam-traction, as the India-rubber tires enable the steamer to go over the softest ground without showing the slightest sign of sinking.

In 1868, extensive experiments were made in Edinburgh to test the powers of the steamer, when it not only hauled several heavily loaded waggons up a very sharp incline, but ran across a soft grass field with the greatest ease, and without leaving the slightest track and, in August 1869, its ploughing capabilities were severely and successfully tried.

On May 25, a further experiment was made in Edinburgh with the steamer and omnibus. The omnibus has only two wheels, and is a handsome and commodious vehicle. It is built to carry sixty-five passengers—twenty inside and forty-four out. The journey, which was to Leith and back, was accomplished without the slightest hitch, and the whole of the party expressed themselves highly satisfied with the performance of Mr. Thomson's ingenious and useful invention.

The Prince of Wales and Princess Louisa at the Opening of t

toria Thames Embankment, July 13, 1870. (See next pages.)

THE VICTORIA THAMES EMBANKMENT

The completion of this great work, the Northern or Middlesex embankment, has afforded much gratification to the Londoners of every class; and such an improvement to the metropolis cannot be seen without pleasure by visitors from any part of the kingdom.

The first idea of the formation of a continuous embankment on the Middlesex side of the river appears to have originated with Sir Christopher Wren upon the occasion of the rebuilding of the metropolis after the Great Fire in 1666. Several schemes having a similar object followed, including those of Sir Frederick Trench and Mr. Martin, the painter. In 1840 Mr. James Walker prepared a plan for the Corporation, and an Act for the formation of a solid embankment, intrusting its execution to the Metropolitan Board of Works, was passed in 1862.

The Victoria Embankment, extending from Westminster Bridge to Black-

Tooley Street Station on the Thames Subway between Tower Hill and Southwark.

friars, is about a mile and a quarter in length; the total area of the land reclaimed from the river being $37\frac{1}{4}$ acres, of which 19 acres are occupied by

Playing Billiards in a Paris Café in Aid of the Territorial Liberation Fund Contributions to pay off the German Conquerors still in Six Eastern Departments, April 1872.

Members of the Working Men's Club and Institute Union on a Conducted Tour of the National Gallery.

carriage and foot ways; 7½ acres have, under the Act of Parliament, been conveyed to the Crown, the societies of the Inner and Middle Temples, and other adjacent landowners; and about 8½ acres are to be devoted to the use of the public, as ornamental grounds.

The main roadway is 100 ft. in width throughout, and is divided into a central carriageway 64 ft. in width, with two footways—that on the land side being 16 ft. wide; and that on the river side 20 ft., along which is planted a row of trees at intervals 20 ft. apart. The public way is protected on the river side by a moulded granite parapet, and on the land side will be divided from the grounds by an ornamental cast-iron railing, instead of the present temporary wooden fencing.

The approaches to the road as now defined will be from Westminster and Blackfriars Bridges, and from Whitehall-place, Villiers, Norfolk, Surrey and Arundel streets. As soon as the railway works are sufficiently advanced to admit of it, the main roadway from

Westminster to Blackfriars will be extended to the Mansion House, thus forming one grand thoroughfare between the Houses of Parliament and the centre of the City. Materials used in the construction works include:—Granite, 650,000 cubic feet; brickwork, 80,000 cubic yards; concrete, 140,000 do.; timber (for cofferdam, &c), 500,000 cubic feet; caissons (for do.), 2500 tons; earth filling, 1,000,000 cubic yards; York paving, 125,000 superficial feet; the total cost of the works when completed is estimated at £1,200,000.

THE OXFORD AND CAMBRIDGE BOAT RACE

"What a day for the Boat Race!" exclaimed thousands last Saturday morning; but bad as the weather was, we determined to venture out. Jumping into a hansom we drove off through a heavy fall of snow that cut against our faces and clung to our hair in the most unpleasant manner. The road seemed comparatively deserted; in fact, until we reached the middle of the Hammersmith Road we did not see a person who seemed going to the race. There we came upon a small vehicle, driven by a stout, elderly gentleman, and containing some three or four ladies, all crouching under umbrellas which were heavy and white with falling snow. Never did a pleasure party appear more miserable; and yet, with that dogged perseverance said to characterise Englishmen, the elderly gentleman kept slowly on his way: he had come out to see the Boat Race, and, wet or dry, he was determined to carry out his purpose.

At the corner of a narrow street we beheld the greatest piece of folly that ever came under our notice: there, in the midst of the drifting sleet, stands a man in the half-frozen slush attempting to sell "penny ices"; but the shivering public turn their backs upon him, preferring to patronise a wiser man who does a thriving trade in baked potatoes, which not only appease the hunger, but warm the fingers. Crowds are pressing forwards to pay the half-penny toll at Hammersmith Bridge. Halfpence are constantly being jerked out of people's hands and sink into the soft mud, lost to their owners for ever. We imagine that an enterprising crossing-sweeper might make a good thing by sweeping that part of the road in the evening. Turning from the Bridge, we stroll down by the river side, where we find stands erected for the accommodation of ladies, very few of whom put in an appearance. On one stand we observe a gentleman, "sad, silent, and alone;" his melancholy condition and despairing attitude giving one the idea that he had asked a party of friends down to enjoy the day, none of whom have come because of the weather. Suddenly we hear a cry of "Here they are—there they go!" followed by great cheering; we inquire the cause, and learn that the boats have passed, Cambridge being ahead. The crowd begins to disperse, amusing themselves with the usual harmless chaff, which is mostly composed of slang sayings and names of music-hall comic songs. At length we get a glimpse of the river, now crowded with small craft of all kinds, amongst which we see a small boat containing a boatman and a very stout gentleman hugging a very stout bottle; from his appearance we should certainly say he had been enjoying the race.

[Cambridge won by two lengths in 21 min., 16 secs.]

[March 1872]

The Night before—Polishing up the Oxford Boat.

The Oxford and Cambridge Boat Race—The Start.

The Oxford and Cambridge Boat Race—Watching the Race.

The Metropolitan Gallery at the Telegraph Office.

THE GPO TELEGRAPH OFFICE

When the Post-Office authorities first took the telegraphs out of the hands of the companies, dire forebodings were uttered, and croakers prognosticated all sorts of inconveniences, and, perhaps, a grand break down. They were disappointed. With a few hitches unavoidable in the carrying out of so great an undertaking the new *régime* has worked admirably, and loud would be the lamentations had we to return to the old system of telegraph offices few and far between, high charges for the country, unmethodical and dilatory delivery of despatches, and a hundred other annoyances. We illustrate here the head office in Telegraph Street, which will give some idea of how the work is carried on in this busiest of Government offices.

Here, then, are concentrated lines from all parts of the United Kingdom and of the Metropolis, connected to all sorts of instruments, from the old-fashioned needle to the newly devised "automatic", worked by clerks of both sexes and all ages, and contained in two enormous rooms, styled respectively the "Provincial" and the "Metropolitan" galleries.

The Metropolitan Gallery contains 217 instruments, and communicates with the District and many of the minor London offices. The staff numbers 256, and, as in the other departments, consists mostly of females. Here, again, is another beneficial feature of the new system—a fresh field has been found for female and what we may term lady-like labour. No less than 539 females are employed at this office, while the district branches are worked by a staff almost entirely composed of young and generally well-educated women. In our sketch one young lady is working a "Morse", while her colleague is busy at a single needle. The working hours are eight, while in addition to her salary every operator is supplied gratis with a daily allowance of tea and bread and butter.

The boys have a kitchen of their own where fire and lights are found them, and they are allowed to cook their own dinners, the materials for which, however, they bring themselves. These little fellows are paid a penny a message—a capital plan for ensuring rapidity of delivery, as their earnings thus depend in a great measure upon their own speed and industry.

The Telegraph Boys' Kitchen.

A Mothers' Meeting: Needlework and a Bible Reading.

Men and women, who would scarcely like to be styled elderly, can nevertheless very well remember when chemical matches were unknown, and when the only implements bearing the names of matches were broad, thin splints of wood tipped with brimstone, and ignited by the laborious agency of flint, steel, and tinder. In those days match-making was carried on upon a very primitive scale, and it was a regular stock joke to style a maker of matches a timber merchant. The joke has now become a grave reality, for the first thing that strikes the eye on entering Messrs. Bryant and May's premises in the Fairfield Road, Bow, is a series of stacks of American spruce timber. This timber is specially selected with a view to superior quality and fineness of grain, and is used for making match-boxes. These boxes are not made at the factory, the wood is sent out to a number of smaller establishments, which return the finished article.

The "splints", that is to say, the wooden bodies of the matches, are also prepared away from the factory, and are brought there in bundles of 2,000 each. Each splint is of the length of two matches. The bundles of splints are placed for a few seconds on a hot plate, so as to char the ends slightly; the ends are then dipped in a pan of melted wax, and again returned to the hot plate for a moment or two. Both ends are subjected to this process, which causes the wood to absorb the wax for a distance of about three quarters of an inch, and renders it easily inflammable. The bundles when dry are brought to the large room shown in our engraving. The workpeople in this department are all young women and girls. Round the sides of the room are the "framers"; at the long central tables are the "boxers". Let us begin by watching one of the framers. She takes one of the bundles of splints, loosens slightly the string which binds it, and rolls it briskly to and fro. This is for the purpose of loosening the splints, which have be-

come stuck together by the wax. She then places the splints by handfuls into a most ingenious machine, worked by steam power, which by the aid of a reciprocating motion, and the impetus offered by a series of needles, arranges some 2,000 matches, which were just before lying higgledy-piggledy, as methodically as soldiers on parade. They are, in fact, fixed tightly in to a frame, as types are fixed in a printer's "chase".

Promethean fire is afforded by the dipping process; and at this point of the process the matches are double-headed, and are twice as long as they ought to be.

They are now ready for the "boxer", who empties the frames on the table. She then gathers up a handful, places them in a grooved rest, and cuts the mass in two with a short knife. By dint of constant experience, one of these handfuls just goes into two boxes, which the operator fills with extraordinary rapidity. One of the boxers informed us, that with steady working she could box thirty-six gross a day. that is to say, 5,184 boxes. This girl earned eighteen shillings a week. . . .

The workpeople are by no means the miserable, emaciated half-starved creatures whom some of our readers might expect to see. On the contrary, they were, as a rule, stout, ruddy, and decently dressed, and the younger children especially seemed full of spirit. At the same time one cannot help reflecting on the monotony of employment which seems to characterise all factory labour. Fancy passing your whole earthly career in guillotining bundles of matches, and then cramming the contents into boxes.

THE BRICKYARDS
OF ENGLAND

The recent deplorable events in Paris show the danger of neglecting the social and moral condition of large masses of the population. The wanton destruction of the Tuileries and other public build-

The Brickyards of England—Children carrying the Clay.

ings of the French capital was but another development of the fierce and vindictive spirit which has so frequently led the brick-makers of Ashton-under-

Life in the Agricultural Districts—Evening in the Labourer's Home.

Lyne and other parts of Lancashire to commit outrages of the most atrocious character. Yet what else could we expect from men who from very infancy have been reared amid the demoralising influences of English brickyards? We allow them to grow up in an ignorant, brutalised, semi-barbarous state, and then are startled to find them frequently destitute of the commonest feelings of humanity. Mr. George Smith, in his pamphlet "The Cry of the Children from the Brickyards of England,"

gives us a close insight into the daily life of the unfortunate little ones; but the details are so painful and repulsive that we would fain hope they were exaggerated, if not untrue. Unfortunately, the statements of Mr. Smith respecting the moral condition of the brickyard children are too strongly corroborated by independent evidence to leave any doubts respecting their credibility.

Children only nine years old have been seen drunk with beer. One boy, a mere child, said that he was made to

drink by the men; at first he refused, but they flung it in his face. The children can often outswear the men themselves. The masters pay the men, who afterwards pay the children, but the latter do not receive their hard-earned wages until the public-house scores of the men have been defrayed. The earnings of the children vary from 3s. to 6s. per week of seventy hours. At Oldbury, a child, *four years old*, was found helping her sister, *aged seven*, to carry clay! Monstrous, is it not?

FEEDING THE YOUNG RAVENS IN GREAT QUEEN STREET

A Friday Dinner at the Boys' Refuge, Great Queen Street.

The young ravens in this case are not birds. Though bipeds, they have no feathers to keep them warm during the cold weather. They are boys and girls, the children of very poor people, and during the winter months 450 of them get a substantial dinner at one o'clock on Fridays at the Boys' Refuge at 8, Great Queen Street, Lincoln's Inn Fields, on condition that they are regular pupils of the ragged schools in

connection with the above institution. They must not miss a day. Thus their intellects are approached through their stomachs. These children are said to be of a class whom the School Board does not reach, being too poor to pay any school fees, though we suspect that if English and Irish parents understood the value of education as well as the Scotch, the school pence would rarely be wanting. The dinner consists of hot

roast meat, potatoes, and a piece of bread, and has been given every winter for six years past. These Friday dinners are highly appreciated. Our artist noticed that a good many of the children kept some of their dinner over to bring home, and although this is against the rules, the authorities are secretly rather glad to see the smuggling carried on for such a praiseworthy purpose.

Meeting of the English Republicans at the ''Hole in the Wall'', Kirby Street, January 1872.

Political Agitators demonstrating in Hyde Park, November 3, 1872, for the Release of Prisoners held for Treason.

THE VELOCIPEDE JOURNEY FROM LONDON TO JOHN O' GROAT'S

The object with which this expedition was undertaken was to show that the bicycle is something more than a mere pleasure-machine, that it is of real practical value, and that it is possible to go from one end of the United Kingdom to the other without the vehicle needing repair or breaking down on the road. Four gentlemen accomplished the whole journey:—Mr. Charles Spencer, with a 48 inch driving wheel; Mr. W. Wood, 52 inch wheel; Mr. George Hunt, 45 inch wheel; and Mr. Charles Leaver, 45 inch wheel. Their enterprise was ren-

dered more arduous by the strong northerly winds which blew almost from the time of their leaving London on Monday, the 2nd June [1873]. They reached John O' Groat's, a distance of 800 miles, at nine P.M., a fortnight after leaving London, and everywhere their advent caused great interest.

EMIGRANTS FOR CANADA

On Board an Emigrant Ship—"Land, ho!"

The *Ganges*, a fine screw-steamer, of 1899 tons register, left the Victoria Docks on April 28, having on board a large party of emigrants. Of the entire number of 761 souls who were on the lists as going by this ship, only four were wanting at the moment the vessel cast. The emigrants were somewhat superior to the usual class, a circumstance partly attributable to the fact that they themselves contributed to the cost of their passage at the rate of £3 per statute adult. The actual cost of sending out this ship-load of emigrants will be rather more than £3400, exclusive of a sum of £1142 which has been advanced to fit out and give the emigrant a start on his landing.

Sleeping Car—going to Bed.

Good night Ma

Dawn—Is it time to get up?

a Smoke

Private-Room

Very refreshing.

Confound it! How the fellow snores.

a quiet Luncheon

Sketches in the New Luxurious Pullman Palace Car on the Midland Railway.

53

The new book which has been most eagerly expected is Mr. H. M. Stanley's narrative of his successful expedition in search of Dr. Livingstone, accompanied by descriptions both of the country traversed by Mr. Stanley himself, as far as the shores of Lake Tanganyka, and of the regions beyond, in the remoter interior of the African Continent, explored by Dr. Livingstone, who has, as he testifies in a letter to his daughter, furnished Mr. Stanley with some materials for this part of the work. "How I Found Livingstone; Travels, Adventures, and Discoveries in Central Africa; Including Four Months' Residence with Dr. Livingstone; by Henry M. Stanley, Travelling Correspondent of the *New York Herald*," is a substantial octavo of 736 pages, illustrated by six maps and plans, twenty-eight full-page engravings on wood, and twenty-five smaller engravings.

The dedication of this volume to Mr. James Gordon Bennett, proprietor of the *New York Herald*, is a due acknowledgement of the "generosity and liberality" shown by that gentleman in sending the expedition, at his sole cost and risk, to find Dr. Livingstone, whose unknown fate was the occasion of so much anxiety, not only in Great Britain but throughout the civilised world. Mr. Stanley was in Spain, reporting what he could see of the revolution there, in October, 1869, when he was summoned by telegram, to meet Mr. Bennett at Paris. Mr. Bennett ordered Mr. Stanley to "go to Africa and find Livingstone," at whatever cost. But we observe that Mr. Bennett did not wish Mr. Stanley to set about this task immediately; he was first to report the inauguration of the Suez Canal, then to go up the Nile, and describe "whatever is worth seeing" in Egypt; then to visit Jerusalem, Constantinople, the Crimea, and the Caucasus; the Euphrates and Bagdad, Persia, and the Caspian Sea. He was to occupy his attention with a variety of different topics in the course of his very circuitous route to India, whence he would pass to Zanzibar. This proves that Mr. Bennett did not think the finding of Dr. Livingstone, alive or dead, was an object of such urgent importance as to be pursued without loss of time. It was not, in fact, until January 1871, a year and two months after he had received this commission from Mr. Bennett in Paris, that Mr. Stanley found his way to Zanzibar, the proper starting-point in search of Livingstone.

Mr. Stanley was the guest in Zanzibar of Captain Francis Webb, the United States Consul. He was introduced to the British Consul, Dr. Kirk, who treated him civilly, but gave him no particular encouragement. Dr. Kirk said that nobody had heard anything definite of Livingstone for more than two years, and he might be dead; "I really think," he added, "the old man should come home now; he is growing old, you know, and if he died the world would lose the benefit of his discoveries." In answer to an inquiry from Mr. Stanley, Dr. Kirk further said that Livingstone was "a very difficult man to deal with generally. Livingstone knows the value of his own discoveries; he is not quite an angel." What actually happened later is a sufficient comment upon this conversation.

Mr. Stanley was employed a whole month at Zanzibar in making preparations for his journey into the interior of Africa. He crossed the strait to Bagamoyo, on the mainland, on Feb. 6. And now began those toilsome wanderings of all but eight months' duration, which were to lead to Livingstone. The route taken by Mr. Stanley has hitherto been untravelled by white men, and lay among tribes of uncouth and barbarous names, which it is hardly possible to fix in the memory—Waroris, Wagogos, Wanyamwezis, Waseguhhas, and Wasagaras—most of them, however, kindly and well-disposed to their visitors, and hardly any positively hostile except in getting every inch of "doti" or cloth that could be squeezed out of them as tribute. Mr. Stanley's stores included eighty-two bales of cloth and some coils of wire and strings of beads, wherewith to pay his way among the barbarous natives.

Before the expedition had proceeded far on its way a plague of stinging flies rendered life hideous, and then came an evil even more formidable. The African rains commenced, and the valley of the Makata river which lay in the route, and had to be crossed, was a mere swamp—a sea of deep, clinging mud. "The donkeys stuck in the mire, as if they were rooted to it. As fast as one was flogged from his stubborn position, prone to the depths fell another."

On the 23rd of June Kwikaru was reached, which with the neighbouring town Taborah appears to be the chief seat of the Arab settlement in Unyanembe. This was a sort of half-way house

Supplies in Jeopardy—"Look out! You drop that box—I'll shoot you."

Mr. Stanley and his Retinue in Africa.

between the coast and Ujiji, and here Mr. Stanley proposed to stay awhile and allow his followers to rest and refresh themselves. But here his troubles waxed thick. War broke out between the Arabs of Unyanembe and a negro chief called Mirambo of Uyoweh, who with his allies possessed the districts through which ran the direct route to Ujiji, so that the passage was barred. The Arabs made great protestations of their ability to beat Mirambo, and so open the road. But after one or two encounters, it became clear that Mirambo had much the best of it; if he was to be beaten at all it would not be for months. So Mr. Stanley, who was during most of this time prostrate with intermittent fever, had to decide between giving up the expedition as impossible for the time, and returning to the coast *re infecta*, or attempting to turn the flank of the hostile territories. He vowed that nothing but death should turn him off his quest, and on the 20th of September, weak and suffering as he was and in spite of the remonstrances and all but mutiny of his men, he broke forth from Unyanembe towards the south, hurried on to Ukononjo, then westward to Kawendi, then northward to Uvinza, then westward to Ujiji. The distance was therefore increased to nearly 600 miles. A week before arriving at Ujiji, Mr. Stanley was told of the actual presence there, at that time, of "a white man, with white hair on his face," who could be no other than Dr. Livingstone.

When Mr. Stanley entered Ujiji on November 3rd, 1871, with the procession of his servants, he found a crowd of people in the street, attracted by the news of his approach. In the centre of a group of Arabs, to the left hand, he perceived a pale, grey-bearded white man, dressed in a shirt or jacket of red serge, with trousers, and wearing on his head a naval cap with a gold band. This was "Dr. Livingstone, I presume!" as Mr. Stanley said in accosting him with the calmness of an ordinary greeting at first sight, as he might have done in New York or London. "Yes," said Dr. Livingstone; and then, joining in quiet talk, they expressed their mutual satisfaction at their meeting, but without any such gestures or looks of strong delight as would have been interpreted by the Arabs and negroes to show that they felt themselves in an unusual position.

It is certain that Dr. Livingstone was very glad to see him, and the stores he brought were most useful, at a time when Livingstone was almost destitute. In his last letter but one, dated Ujiji December 18, 1871, Dr. Livingstone writes:—"A vague rumour reached Ujiji in the beginning of last month that an Englishman had come to Unyanembe with boats, horses, men, and goods in abundance. It was in vain to conjecture who this could be, and my eager enquiries were met by answers so contradictory that I began to doubt if any stranger had come at all. But one day— I cannot say which, for I was three weeks too fast in my reckoning— my man, Susi, came dashing up in great excitement, and gasped out, 'An Englishman coming; see him!' and off he ran to meet him. The American flag at the head of the caravan told me the nationality of the stranger. It was Henry M. Stanley, sent to obtain correct information about me, if living; and, if dead, to bring home my bones. The kindness was extreme, and made my whole frame thrill with excitement and

This Engraving, for which I supplied the materials, represents my m...
at Ujiji, Lake Tanganyika; and is as correct as if the scene...

with Dr. Livingstone
been photographed.

57

Dr. Livingstone and Mr. Stanley receiving Newspapers in Central Africa.

gratitude. I had been left nearly destitute by the moral idiot Shereef selling off all my goods for slaves and ivory for himself. My condition was sufficiently forlorn, for I had but a very few articles of barter left of what I had taken the precaution to leave here, in case of extreme need. The strange news Mr. Stanley had to tell to one for years out of communication with the world was quite reviving. Appetite returned, and in a week I began to feel quite strong . . ."

Mr. Stanley was entertained in August 1872 at dinner at the Garrick Club, where he described his journey and the condition in which he found the great explorer. The doctor, he said, had been so long without news from the civilised world that he refused to open his budget of letters until, under the historical verandah, he had listened to all the news of both worlds, and he at length retired to his hut to digest his long-delayed missives from friends. During the many, many days they travelled together, Mr. Stanley never heard an impatient word from Dr. Livingstone; and it was only at the sea coast that the journalist again realised how much more enterprise was exhibited by his profession than by dilettante travellers,

whose object seemed to be to shoot down elephants. Nothing could exceed the tenderness of the respect which Mr. Stanley throughout evinced for the courage of Livingstone, who, as he truly said, had in his many wanderings been touched by the hand of God; nor could anything be more engaging than his earnest relation of the most moving tale which has ever excited all the nations of the civilised world.

The information which has come to hand during the last week of the whereabouts, the condition, the past movements, and future purposes of Dr. Livingstone, the great geographical explorer of Central Africa, is of the highest interest. It comes to us—strange to say—from an American source. What the expedition organised by the Royal Geographical Society failed to accomplish, Mr. Stanley, representing nothing more than the energy and the pecuniary credit of the *New York Herald*, has had the good fortune to compass, single-handed. It has been said, with great truth, that a council of war never fights. It may also be affirmed that, with few exceptions, a perilous expedition is usually much more effectively carried out by a single individual

than by an organised party—always assuming, of course, that the intellectual qualifications required for the work are not largely unequal. Be this, however, as it may—and perhaps it would be presumptuous to draw a general inference from particular cases—we are bound to congratulate Mr. Gordon Bennett, the proprietor of the *New York Herald*, and Mr. Stanley, his commissioner, upon having been instrumental in discovering Dr. Livingstone, and, by the timely sympathy and support they extended to him, having snatched him, as it were, from the very jaws of despondancy.

Let us for a moment or two look at what Dr. Livingstone himself has done during the five years that he has been lost to civilised society. Of his personal adventures we know but little, save that he was baffled by the cowardice and treachery of his native servants when he was within sight of the object of his expedition, and that he had to return to the spot at which Stanley found him, a mere "ruckle of bones", as he has pathetically as well as picturesquely expressed it. Six hundred miles of the watershed of Central Africa he succeeded in exploring, and has now little more than a hundred miles to

A Revival of the Old Coaching Days: The Four-in-Hand Club, St. James's Street.

complete his task. Within that small portion of unknown land, which is now the only unsolved mystery relating to the river Nile, the enterprising traveller expects to find a full confirmation of the old Egyptian traditions handed down to us by the Father of History [Herodotus], and until very recently supposed to be rather a romance of imagination than a description corresponding with the actual facts of the case. A very considerable extent of country, casting light on the main geographical features of Central Africa, has already been explored. Judging from the tenor of Livingstone's letters to Mr. Gordon Bennett, the main difficulty of access to the interior lies in the slave trade carried on by Arab Moslems from Zanzibar. His account of the races to be met with, scattered over the watershed to which we have alluded, indicates that, apart from the deteriorating influences of slavery, the inhabitants of Central Africa have a kind of civilisation little dreamt of by European anthro-

pologists, and that the whole country which they people is rich, beyond ordinary supposition, in those resources which stimulate and repay commercial enterprise. The natives are not unfriendly to strangers, further than they have been provoked to inhospitality by slaving expeditions. At any rate, Livingstone himself received from them kindly attention to him, which seems to have commended them to his sympathising remembrance. He has written of them to Mr. Bennett in rather warm and eulogistic terms, and he has certainly opened up a prospect for the future which, if it be not blighted by the tolerated ravages of the slave trade, will one day present features of deep interest, social, moral, and probably religious, of the most surprising and gratifying kind.

It may be asked whether these geographical expeditions are worth their cost. Our readers, we imagine, will not require any elaborate reply to such a question. Dr. Livingstone is but one of a

noble and intrepid band of travellers whose explorations have not only solved geographical problems of the deepest interest, but have pioneered the way into unknown regions for the subsequent entrance of commerce, civilisation, knowledge, and religion. As in the western world Anglo-American enterprise usually followed the paths taken by the trappers, so on the African continent the expeditions of scientific travellers and the somewhat less glorious adventures of sportsmen may be confidently expected to result in that well-founded knowledge which commonly lies at the basis of human intercourse. "Ignorance," the proverb says, "is the parent of crime." Men are separated from each other by their ignorance of each other's ways far more than by any natural barrier. It is to such men as Dr. Livingstone that the world is indebted for the constant growth of scientific information, and for those benefits to mankind which almost invariably accompany it.

The Eton v Harrow Match at Lord's: Hoisting the Victor.

ETON v HARROW

Everyone who takes an interest in cricket, and many to whom drives, cuts and leg-hits are mysteries, have read an account of the great School Match which was played at Lords on Friday and Saturday last [July 8 and 9, 1870], resulting, after an exciting struggle, in a victory for Eton by twenty-one runs. When the last Harrow wicket went, and the Etonians greeted their victory with cheer on cheer, then followed that scene without which no school match is complete. A rush is made to the pavilion, cheers and counter cheers ring out, those who have borne themselves well are now borne by others and carried in triumph round the wickets; the man who has made a good score, or bowled good wickets, or made a clever catch at a critical point of the game, is seized upon by enthusiastic admirers, hustled and pulled and cheered in a way that must be more complimentary than pleasing. All the boys of Harrow have doubtless accounted for their defeat in a way satisfactory to themselves, and have resolved to win another time; and the boys of Eton have as satisfactorily proved that they could not have been beaten, with the advantage of accomplished facts to appeal to.

A HORSE DOWN

[Between 1872 and 1874 a financial adventurer named Grant spent some £28,000 in laying out Leicester Square; an equestrian statue of George I was then removed. Lawsuits resulted in his bankruptcy, but the gardens, with busts of Reynolds, Hogarth &c are part of his scheme.]

In a certain district of London there is a famous horse statue (we do not use the word "equestrian" because equestrian implies a rider, who in this instance has disappeared). The fame of that statue marvellously resembles infamy, not from its own demerits, for it is not worse than many other London statues, but because, owing to the litigation of contending proprietors, Leicester Square has now become a howling wilderness, although it was a nice place in Sir Joshua Reynolds's time, and a pleasant enough spot even in our own time, when the ladies used to go bonnet-chasing in Cranbourn Alley. On the north side of the Square there is rather a treacherous piece of asphalte, treacherous we say, because it is so short that the horses have no time to get accustomed to it, and consequently the phenomenon of "A Horse Down" is of frequent occurrence. In our artist's sketch the horse is not so hopelessly down as he sometimes is, when he lies as if dead, and when one man goes and unfastens the traces while another holds his head, lest he should suddenly let fly with his hind legs. In the case before us it is rather a question of deranged equilibrium, and if those two or three volunteer philanthropists will only hang on behind, the horse will be pulled up on his legs willy-nilly: and the old lady whom the policeman is reassuring will be able to proceed on her journey.

The Two Hours' Channel Crossing

The Horrors of the "Middle-Passage".

Sunday on the Union Pacific Railway:
A Methodist Service in an American "Travelling Drawing-Room".

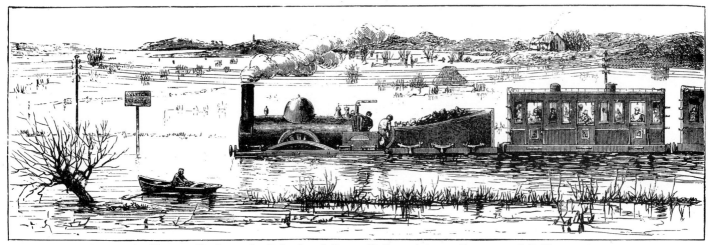

An Express Train on the Bristol and Exeter Railway between Durston and Bridgwater.

Though during the last few days [November 27, 1875] there had been a rapid subsidence of the waters at Oxford, at the time our sketch was taken the Great Western Railway was flooded to such an extent that the artist paddled a canoe along the line for quite half a mile. The road from Oxford to Abingdon was also deeply flooded. Passengers from London left the trains at Radley Station and were conveyed in vehicles of all descriptions through the floods to Oxford. He saw from his canoe, in the course of a few minutes, a coach and four, with three horses trotting behind for changing, about five "Hansoms", and several flys and cabs.

A NEW STEAM CHANNEL FERRY

A trial of the model of a proposed Steam Channel Ferry, designed by Mr. H. A. Egerton, took place on the afternoon of February 19, 1876, on the Serpentine, Hyde Park. The object of the inventor is to provide a model of transit which shall remain steady in the heaviest weather ever experienced in

Trial of a New Steam Channel Ferry on the Serpentine.

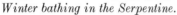
Winter bathing in the Serpentine.

Summer bathing in the Serpentine.

the Channel. Mr. Egerton's model represents three pontoon rafts, composed of cylinders tapering towards each end, and connected by transverse girders. On these latter is a deck, beyond which at either end project the pontoons, which are fitted amidships with huge paddle-wheels. To convey whole trains across the Channel, and secure them against pitching and rolling, it is only necessary, according to Mr. Egerton, to have a vessel made on this plan, and big enough to defy the highest Channel waves, which never exceed 14 feet. Such a vessel would be 600 ft. long and 228 ft. wide. Her estimated speed is 15 knots an hour, and her cost when fully equipped for service 110,000 *l.* The inventor claims that a vessel of this type and dimensions would sail as steadily in such a sea as if she were lying at anchor in harbour. The model sailed well, and showed that it could be easily steered by means of the paddles.

CAPTAIN BOYTON'S GLORIOUS DEFEAT

On Saturday last [April 10, 1875] Captain Paul Boyton attempted to cross the English Channel in the Merriman life-saving suit; and was persuaded eventually to give up before the feat was accomplished, but not until he had been in the water fifteen hours, covering over fifty miles, and being within six miles of the French coast when he went, against his will, on board the accompanying steam-tug. The life-dress consists of a solid india-rubber tunic, with headpiece and gloves attached, and a pair of pantaloons terminating in boots. It is secured with a water-tight joint at the waist. The wearer is rendered buoyant by the inflation of five air-chambers. The

Captain Boyton's Voyage across the Channel.

headpiece has a small opening which only exposes his eyes, nose, and mouth.

Captain Boyton, a native of Pittsburg, Pennsylvania, is Captain of the New Jersey Life-Saving Service. He was not in first rate condition for his adventure; and at the last moment there was an awkward delay in donning his india-rubber suit, through the misfit of some of his underclothing. It was reckoned that, by starting at three sharp, Captain Boyton would be carried up Channel by the flood to an easterly point, whence he could run down Channel with the ebb on the French side of the long shoal known as the Ridge, or the Colbart,

until the tide should again turn, and carry him ashore somewhere between Boulogne and Cape Grisnez. Twenty minutes past three, however, was the time the start was delayed to; and it is to the loss of this important twenty minutes that Captain Boyton's ultimate failure can be attributed. Clad in his grey suit, and furnished only with a flask of brandy, a fog-horn, a small axe in a sheath, and his canoe paddle, Captain Boyton glided into the water with the ease of a sea-lion, turned on his back, and quickly propelled himself out of Dover harbour with his paddle, progressing feet first, as usual, and

paddled serenely on, only sounding a cheerful note on his fog-horn when those aboard the steam-tug had completely lost sight of him. A little later he called for his sail. What looked like the small mainsail of a miniature yacht was then fixed into a tube fastened to the sole of his boot; and, with set sail, he rode more fleetly than ever over the billows . . . At six o'clock the wind became brisker, the weather was hazy, and it threatened to be a rough night. Land was not in sight, and Captain Boyton, manfully protesting, at length gave up his courageous undertaking sorely against his will.

CAPTAIN WEBB'S ATTEMPT TO SWIM ACROSS THE CHANNEL

Hot Coffee by Moonlight.

It seems but the other day that an Illustration was published of Captain Boyton enjoying a cigar in the middle of the English Channel. Buoyed up by his life-saving dress, the gallant young American could not have had on that occasion half the difficulty that Captain Webb had in taking a draught of coffee during his Channel swim in the nude on Thursday, August 12th. The start took place from the Admiralty Pier, Dover,

at a minute and a half before five in the afternoon. The intrepid young English sailor rode bravely over the waves, treading water while he took refreshment, and pluckily swam for six hours and forty-nine minutes in his unsuccessful attempt to swim across the English Channel . . . He persevered till a quarter to twelve, when the increasing roughness of the sea made it clear that his daring attempt would be fruitless in

that stormy weather. It has been announced that Captain Webb will make a second endeavour to swim across the Channel; but it is to be hoped that he may be dissuaded from again attempting so hopeless and utterly useless a task. We are strongly of the opinion that the various antagonistic tides and currents of the Channel will ever present any man from swimming across without artificial aid.

Lord Gifford's Scouts setting fire to a Village.

[Great Britain and the Ashanti had been hostile since 1863; in 1869 the Ashanti had captured a party of missionaries in Togoland, and in 1873 an Ashanti offensive had defeated the Denkera and Fanti states. In February 1874 British troops led an offensive against the Ashanti and captured and destroyed Kumasi.]

When, not long since, we touched upon the prospects of the expeditionary force in Ashantee, founding our anticipations upon the tenor of Sir Garnet Wolseley's latest despatch, we assumed the probability of his reaching Coomassie without further serious opposition, and of his obtaining from King Koffee Kalkalli a satisfactory treaty of peace. Things, however, did not turn out in accordance with general anticipation. The Ashantee Monarch was employing craft in the hope of entrapping the foe whom his own ambition had provoked. His Embassies were sent, one after the other, to the headquarters of Sir Garnet Wolseley with the simple view of gaining time. The interval was energetically employed in collecting his armed followers. He was determined to fight for

his capital—perhaps, we may say, for his Crown and Kingdom.

Sir Garnet Wolseley, even if he did not detect the snare which cunning had spread for him, was firmly bent upon pushing forward to Coomassie without an hour's unnecessary delay. His despatches tell how he reached that place "after five days' hard fighting", how he occupied it with his little army, how he was again beset with artful messages from the frightened King, and how at length he was driven to the conclusion that no reliance whatever could be placed upon that Sovereign's word. There was no alternative left but the infliction of summary and severe punishment upon the wily foe. Successive tornadoes had given impressive warning to Sir Garnet and his colleagues that a few days' stay where they were might put an insurmountable obstacle in the way of their return to the coast. Rain had fallen heavily; the rivers which they had crossed on their march northward were rapidly rising. The roads were becoming slippery, swampy, and in places nearly impassable. To temporise would have been madness;

to return without leaving behind some visible and impressive evidence of the superiority of British power would have been to forego the main objects of the expedition. Reluctantly, but without the least hesitation as to the duty which devolved upon him, Sir Garnet Wolseley gave instructions for the destruction of Coomassie by fire. The palace of the King was mined, and the city was set fire to in several quarters. The troops evacuated while it was still in flames. The work of destruction was complete. Captain Sartorius, with an escort of twenty men detached from Glover's force, a few miles to the east of the city, passed through the ruins a day or two afterwards, and saw not a living soul had remained on the spot. The lesson seems to have told on the mind of the King as nothing else could have done. Enraged as he was by the losses he had sustained, and apprehending further disaster from the advance of Glover's force, he sent messages to Sir Garnet Wolseley, this time with an instalment of a war indemnity in their hands, to request the immediate countermanding of the further march of the troops under

Glover, and to express his readiness to sign any treaty which Sir Garnet might deem suitable and necessary. Thus has ended a war forced upon us by wanton aggression on the part of the Ashantees. The programme of Sir Garnet Wolseley has been realised in all its parts. He has done what he said he would do; he has done it all within the brief period which he assigned for its execution. Our troops and our tars are now on their passage home, and may be expected off our own coasts in a few days. They will, no doubt, receive the distinction which they have deserved. They have borne the flag of England through a pestilential country to a capital deemed by most to be beyond reach of European power. They have shed new lustre, by their discipline, their courage, and their success, upon the name and fame of the nation which they represented. If, to a large extent, the war was, as Lord Derby characterised it, "an engineer's war", we have yet the consolation derived from the thought that it has been admirably conducted, and has resulted in a triumphant achievement of the end for which it was undertaken.

HOMECOMING

The British soldiers and their skilful General, lately employed in the chastisement of a barbarian King of black warriors in West Africa, have returned victorious to receive a hearty welcome and just applause from their fellow-

The Naval Brigade clearing the Streets of Coomasie.

countrymen of the United Kingdom. The arrival of several troopships or transports conveying these regiments home from Cape Coast Castle has kept Portsmouth and London in pleasing excitement since March 19. At Portsmouth, the Mayor and Corporation, in their robes of civic dignity, presented an address of welcome. The troops, wearing their soiled grey tunics and trousers and pith helmets, as during the late campaign, instead of their regimental uniform, marched through the High-street amidst the cheers and hat-waving or handkerchief-fluttering salutes of a great crowd of people. At the railway station they were entertained with a plain luncheon of bread and cheese and beer, provided by the town Corporation. . . . Her Majesty the Queen sent an inviting command to Sir Garnet Wolseley to visit her at Windsor Castle, and the Lord Mayor of London has invited him and all the officers of the Ashantee Expedition to a banquet at the Mansion House next Tuesday, April 1. [1874]

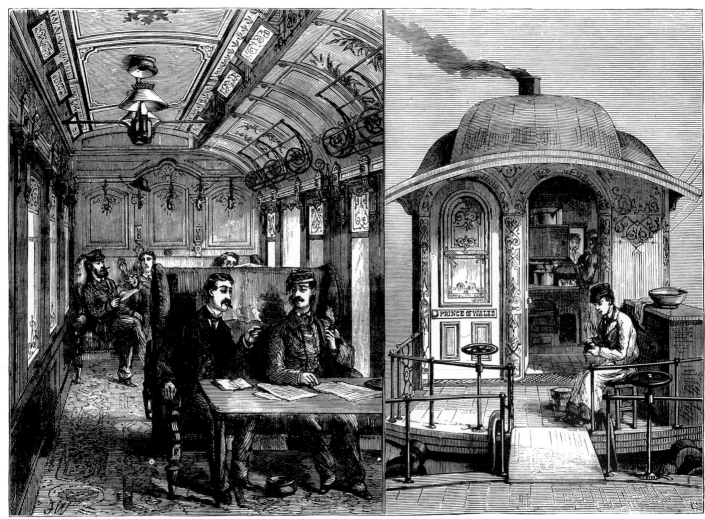

Smoking Saloon and Kitchen, Great Northern Railway.

THE PULLMAN DINING CAR

The Great Northern Railway Company has been the first in England to adopt this comfortable American system, which has been in daily operation since Nov. 1, in one train each way between Leeds and London. The Pullman Palace Car Company, whose sleeping and drawing-room cars are in use upon several English and Scottish railways, have provided for the Great Northern line a handsome and convenient new carriage. It was constructed at Detroit, in the United States, at a cost of £3000. It is fifty-two feet in length, eight feet in breadth, and runs upon eight wheels. It comprises a dining-saloon, in the middle, a kitchen behind, and a smoking-room in front, with steward's pantry, ladies' dressing-room, gentlemen's lavatory, cupboards, and stoves. The dining-room has six tables, three on each side; there are ten easy chairs, large, well-stuffed, and covered with crimson velvet, each revolving on a solid pivot. The ladies' dressing-room, which adjoins this, has a stove, enclosed in a metal-lined wooden cupboard. The sides or walls of the saloon are of American black walnut, decorated with veneer of French walnut. The smoking-room has two tables, and seats for nine persons. There are electric bells to summon the attendants, who are the cook, the steward or waiter, and the boy of the smoking-room. The refreshments, including wines, are supplied by Pullman's Company at ordinary hotel dinner charges. Any first-class passenger on the line may use this Pullman Car on payment of half-a-crown over and above the ordinary fare for his journey. The up train, to which this car is attached, starts from Leeds at ten a.m., and arrives at King's Cross, London, at two p.m. The down train by which the car returns leaves King's Cross at 5.30 p.m., reaching Leeds at 10.10 p.m. So that a Leeds man, by this arrangement, may start from home after his usual breakfast, fortify himself with lunch at one o'clock, take three hours for his business in London, dine comfortably at six or seven o'clock, and get to bed in his own house an hour before midnight. This seems to be just what one should want.

... When his Royal Highness was at the grand open-air treat given to 11,000 native school children, in the Oval Meadow, near the Government Offices [on November 10], he was greeted with a peculiar but graceful compliment on the part of the fair sex. A beautiful Parsee girl, attired in pink satin, whose name is Miss Dhunbaee Ardasser Wadia, came up to his Royal Highness and Sir Philip Wodehouse, laden with wreaths or garlands of jasmine. She held up one of them before the Prince, who at first took it with his hand, mistaking her intention; upon which she offered another wreath to the Governor. Sir Philip, more experienced in these matters, bowed his head, and allowed her to place the garland over his neck. When the Prince saw this, he smiled and attempted to hang his own garland round his neck in a similar fashion; but Miss Wadia promptly undertook and performed the little office, after which she gave him a bouquet of roses, jasmine, and yellow Christmas flowers. A band of Hindu girls then sang an anthem, in the Mahratta language, followed by Parsee girls, with the same in the language of Guzerat, expressing their joy at the Prince's arrival and their fervent wishes for his happiness. . . .

. . . The arches and floral, or rather horticultural, decorations of Ceylon were of a kind peculiar to the island and illustrative of its fertility. One of the arches at Colombo was also illustrative of the island and of its zoology. The elephants were produced by a framework covered with leaves and moss and creeping plants. The shape of the animals has been well carried out, so much so that, when sketching, our Artist saw a horse shy as it came up.

. . . The Prince's hunting party in the Terai of Kumaon and Nepaul moved across the open country with fifty-two elephants in line, killing boar, deer, and partridge till it reached the edge of the jungle, where it was expected to find tigers. The jungle evidently held large game, and presently sight was caught of two dark forms for a moment, but it was some time before one of these became visible and was fired at and killed. It was a fine sloth bear, 6½ ft. long, weighing 250 lb. . . .

[November 1875–March 1876]

(Top of the page) The School Children's Fete, Bombay. (Above) Arch at Colombo, Ceylon, on the Occasion of the Royal Visit.

Shooting: The Critical Moment.

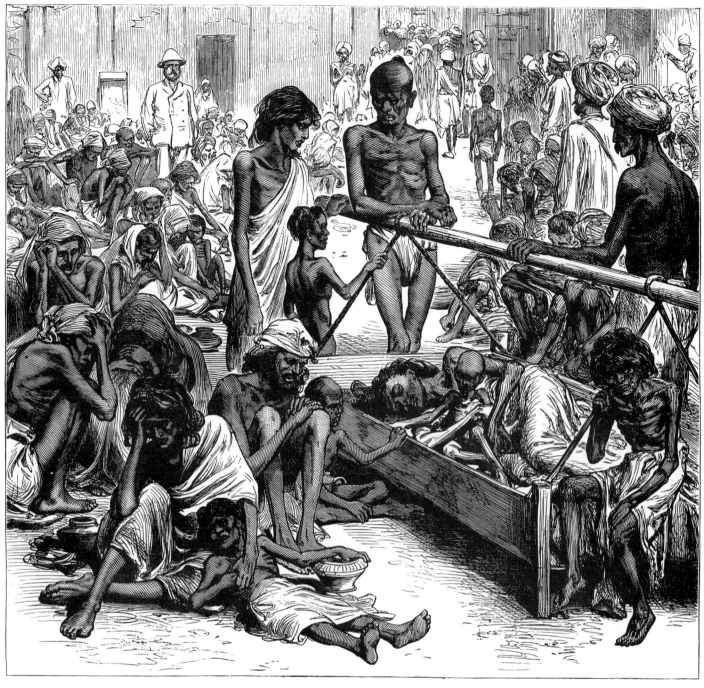

FAMINE IN INDIA

The dark cloud of the Madras Famine is at length beginning to exhibit a silver lining. Plenteous rain has now fallen in many of the worst famine districts, agricultural work is active, and future prospects are hopeful. People are rapidly deserting the relief works and hurrying away to their homes. A few weeks will make a great difference to the panic-stricken people, who had been reduced to so starving a condition previous to admission that considerable time must elapse before they are able to work. There can be no reasonable doubt that the tide of the great calamity has been turned; but vast numbers of those who survive the actual famine must still succumb from their enfeebled condition,

the effect of rain and cold nights. The total number on the relief works in Madras is 587,228, showing a decrease from the previous week of 72,466 [October 20, 1877].

FAMINE IN CHINA

The crops having failed in the province of Shantung, great distress has prevailed amongst the people there for the last few months. But in addition to hunger they have suffered intensely from the cold, the winter being always severe in that part of China. Immense numbers of refugees have been flocking southwards —this place (Chinkiang) attracting a good many. They have erected straw huts around about here in every shel-

tered spot, and live in the most wretched manner. Many of them are only too ready to part with their little ones to procure sustenance. Our illustration represents what our artist actually saw at Chinkiang, a mother conveying her children to town to be sold. They were all fine healthy looking little things.

A Roman Catholic missionary thus describes the distress in the district of Lin Kin:—"In the almost deserted villages you see but exhausted, cadaverous faces. How many families have become totally extinct through starvation; how many have gone elsewhere, after having sold their all at any price, without hope of return? But there is something worse. How many fathers of families who once lived honourably have committed suicide in order to avoid the ignominy of begging, all their family following their dreadful example! How many woe-stricken women have been sold by their fathers, brothers, and husbands to unknown people, till in some places you see hardly any females left! . . .'   [September 13, 1877]

CLERKENWELL HOUSE

The large prison, belonging to the county of Middlesex, in Coldbath-fields, Clerkenwell is designed to contain nearly two thousand male offenders, under penal sentence for different terms, from one week to two years.

The Coldbath-fields prison is seldom quite full; 1,750 was the number actually there when the sketch was made which is now presented to our readers; but the average is 1,600 adults and 100 juveniles. There are two classes, with different kinds or degrees of hard labour. Those of the first class are kept to the tread-wheel, the motion of which is utilised for grinding wheat and pumping water from the well to a tank which supplies the prison. Those of the second class are employed in oakum picking, and in mat, brush, and basket-making, or in shoemaking, tailoring, and other trades, if they are fit to learn such useful arts;

Famine in China—Children for sale at Shantung.

besides washing and cleaning the premises. The treadwheel is a huge double machine, erected on both sides of a long gallery, the "wheel-yard", where 684 prisoners are assembled at a time. Half of these, namely, 342 men and boys— are upon the steps of the wheel for ten minutes, while the other half sit down and rest; so they take their turns, one set relieving another, throughout the working time of the day, which is six hours and a half. The actual exertion for each person is, therefore, limited to three hours and a quarter; and those who have tried it say that it is not more fatiguing than to climb an ordinary

The Needle-room at the Clerkenwell House of Correction.

ladder. The work of picking oakum is rather painful to delicate fingers, but becomes easy after a few days.

Our illustration shows the work of tailoring. The prisoners are constantly watched, and are forbidden to speak a word to each other when assembled for work or dinner; even a detected glance or sign would be severely punished. Each person is locked up at night in a solitary cell.

A Suggestion for a Flying Machine.

HOW TO REACH THE POLE

All attempts to reach the North Pole have, up to the present time, resulted in failure, but a novel plan has been suggested by Commander Cheyne, R.N., to employ balloons. Three balloons, connected in the manner shown, would carry six men, besides three tons weight of gear, boat-cars, stores, provisions, tents, sledges, dogs, compressed gas, and ballast. The triangular framework, connecting the balloons would be fitted with foot-ropes, so that the occupants could go from one balloon to another in the same manner as sailors lie out upon the yards of a ship, and the balloon would be equi-poised by means of bags of ballast suspended from this frame-work, and hauled to the required positions by ropes. Trail ropes would be attached to the balloons, so as to prevent their ascent above a certain height (about 500 feet), at which elevation they would be balanced in the air, the spare ends of the ropes trailing over the ice . . . Commander Cheyne proposes that the balloons should start about the end of May, on the curve of a wind circle, of known diameter, ascertained approximately by meteorological observations. It is estimated that, with a knowledge of the diameter of the wind circle, and the known distance from the Pole, the balloons could be landed within at least twenty miles of the long-wished-for goal. . . . [1877]

The Proposed Polar Expedition—How to reach the North Pole by Balloons.

On April 15 the balloon called the *Zenith* started from the Villette Gas Works, carrying M. Gaston Tissandier, a well-known aeronaut, and editor of the journal *La Nature*, Captain Sivel, a naval officer, who had previously made 151 ascents, and M. Croce-Spinelli, the author of several valuable treatises on aerial navigation. All went well for the first hour and a-half, but in ten minutes, at the altitude of $3\frac{3}{4}$ miles above the earth, the aeronauts began to be distressed, their hands were frozen, and breathing became difficult . . . Suddenly all three became powerless, and fell senseless. It was then just 1.30 P.M. At 2.8 P.M. M. Tissandier and his companions regained their senses, found the balloon to be rapidly descending, and in order to stay the descent threw out quantities of ballast, and an instrument termed the *aspirateur*, which weighed 80 pounds. The balloon once more ascended, and again the occupants became unconscious. At 3.15 P.M. M. Tissandier regained his senses, found the balloon to be descending at a frightful speed, and his two companions lying dead at the bottom of the car, their faces being black and their mouths covered with blood. Rousing himself

The "Zenith" with the three Aeronauts.

with difficulty, he managed to cut the anchor adrift, open the gas valve, and after some time the balloon was finally caught and held by a tree at Ciron, a village in the Department of Indre. The cause of the catastrophe is mainly attributed to throwing out so heavy a weight as the *aspirateur*. . .   [1875]

The fatal Descent at Ciron.

Bound for India—Scene at the departure of a Peninsul

...d Oriental Company's Steamer from Southampton.

The arrival of Dr. Schliemann in London, and his address to the Society of Antiquaries, must increase the amount of public interest already felt in his successful explorations of the sites of ancient classic history, or early traditions of romantic events in Greece, celebrated by the epic and tragic poets of that highly gifted nation. His laudable endeavours, and large pecuniary sacrifices, at his own private risk, to carry on these laborious and costly researches appear more worthy of note, from the circumstance that he is not a man trained to the profession of literary and academic scholarship; that he has never been a professor of any of the German or other Universities; but that his youth and part of his manhood, in Hamburg and in London, were incessantly occupied with commercial business. Since his retirement, within the last few years, he has devoted nearly all his time, and a great deal of his money, to the self-imposed task of examining the places associated with the chief actions related in Homer's "Iliad", and those of collateral importance described in the narratives or dramatic compositions of other Greek poets. His success in the Troad, or that district of the coast of Asia Minor, just below the Dardanelles, where two or three different sites had been alleged for the famous city of Ilium or Troy, was, perhaps, the commencement of a new era in the progress of classical archaeology. . . . Dr. Schliemann claims to have found the relics of an actual Troy, with the palace and tomb of Priam, and those of Agammemnon at Mycenae; and insists,

with his usual enthusiasm, upon the reality which belongs to everything which Homer describes in relation to Troy, and that we are now getting revealed to our eyes what the poet was familiar with when he wrote. . . .

(Top of the page) Dr. Schliemann and the Society of Antiquaries. (Above) Exhibition of the Mycenae Treasure.

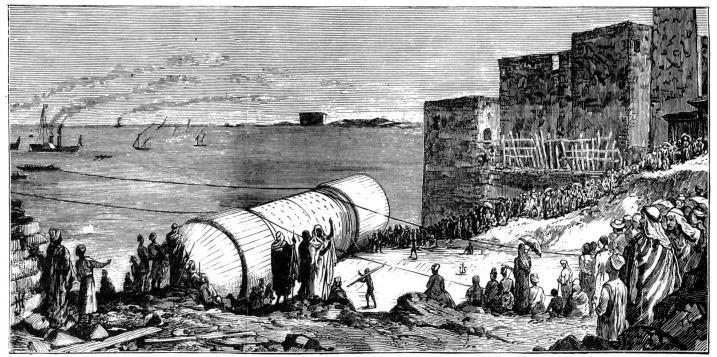

Launch of the Obelisk at Alexandria.

Egypt, September 22, 1877. A telegram to the *Daily News* states that the vessel which is to bring Cleopatra's Needle to England has been fitted for sea, and that she would probably start on her voyage near the close of this week. The cigar-shaped vessel was designed by Mr. John Dixon; it was built round the obelisk. Arrangements have been completed for the steamer *Olga* to tow the iron case containing the obelisk from Alexandria to England. The case has been fitted up with accommodation for four men, whose duty will be to steer the mass in the wake of the steamer and thus minimise the tension on the tow lines.

October 20, 1877. Last Sunday there sprang up a gale which raged in the Bay of Biscay. So high did the seas run off Cape Finisterre (as reported by the captain of the steam-ship *Olga*) that the *Cleopatra* cylinder-ship had to be cast off by the *Olga*, which had towed it from Alexandria. At six on Sunday evening a tremendous sea threw the *Cleopatra* on her beam ends. The mast was then cut away, and every effort made to right her, but without success. Signals of distress were made by the *Cleopatra*, and at ten o'clock, the wind having abated, six men from the *Olga* pluckily went to the rescue. They succeeded in reaching the *Cleopatra*, but before they could render any assistance their boat was swept away and seen no more. The *Olga* went on an unsuccessful search for the men, and then returned to where the *Cleopatra* had been cut adrift, the Maltese crew having been

previously saved by the boat being hauled to her from the *Olga* by means of a rope. The loss of Cleopatra's Needle was, however, but temporary. We are glad to learn that the *Fitzmaurice* steamer, from Middlesburg for Valencia, fell in with and recovered the cylinder vessel ninety miles north of Ferrol.

Abandonment of Cleopatra's Needle in the Bay of Biscay.

January 26, 1878. The iron cylinder-ship *Cleopatra* arrived safely in the Thames on Monday last. It was towed by a steam-tug, in six days, from where it had been left since October last, after having been cast off in a storm by the *Olga*, which had brought it from Egypt. The latter part of the voyage has now been successfully accomplished by the aid of the *Anglia*, a powerful steam-tug belonging to Mr. Watkins of Lombard-street. The expenses of bringing the obelisk to England are defrayed by the splendid liberality of Mr. Erasmus Wilson, the eminent surgeon, who has received from the Princess of Wales, a gracious message in recognition of his generous gift to the country.

The controversy about the best site for the obelisk in London has not yet been ended. Mr. Erasmus Wilson has proposed the centre of the ornamental garden, adjacent to Old Palace-yard and to St Margaret's-churchyard, Westminster, sometimes called Parliament-square, where a wooden model of the obelisk, equal to it in size, has been erected to show the effect.

February 16, 1878. On Saturday last, the obelisk vessel was brought out into the Thames and placed between two steam-tugs, the *Trojan* and *Ajax*, which were fastened alongside of her, to hold her in a straight course and prevent her swinging to either side of the channel. The *Cleopatra* has her mast unshipped because of the bridges, but Captain Carter displayed the Union Jack, the burgee, and the red ensign. Other vessels joined in a sort of procession, which came up the river with high tide, and reached Westminster Bridge about half-past one in the afternoon. The *Cleopatra* was moored, or lashed to a dredging vessel, about one hundred yards above Westminster Bridge, near the Lambeth side of St. Thomas's Hospital, opposite the Houses of Parliament. Many visitors have been admitted to inspect this curious vessel, and to look at a portion of the surface of the inclosed obelisk, for which purpose an iron plate has been removed from the deck. It now rests with the Metropolitan Board of Works, unless Parliament take up the matter, to decide whether the obelisk shall be erected on the Thames Embankment in front of Adelphi-terrace. The site originally proposed, where the wooden model obelisk stood, in the garden of "Parliament-square", was found in-admissible, because of the underground railway.

August 10, 1878. The Egyptian obelisk is now visible to all passers by on the Thames Embankment, and will soon be reared aloft upon its pedestal, at the riverside steps opposite Adelphi-terrace. It still rests in a horizontal position, but stripped of the iron-plate casing that formed the vessel in which its adventurous voyage was performed, upon a solid timber framework over the granite base, 16 ft. square and 6 ft. high, but rising only 4 ft. above the level of the Embankment, supporting the pedestal and the two plinths at the sides. The operations of lifting the obelisk to the required height, then depressing one end so as to render it perpendicular, and finally planting its lower end upon the pedestal, will soon commence, and are expected to require several weeks before all is complete.

The plan for raising may be here described. The column will be fitted with a powerful iron jacket as near the centre of gravity as is wanted; and this jacket has two massive iron trunnions, just like the trunnions of a great gun. These trunnions will rest on two wrought iron girders of great strength;

The Cylinder Ship Cleopatra, *with the Obelisk, at Westminster Bridge.*

and the whole will then resemble a monster cannon on a slide without wheels. Each of the four main uprights of the staging consists of six sticks of timber, each 1 ft. square. The iron jacket, consisting of plates and girders, is being fixed round the central portion of the obelisk. The wrought-iron "strap" which will pass under the butt end of the obelisk from two opposite sides of this jacket (in order to prevent the monolith from slipping out) is of $\frac{3}{4}$-in. metal and 24 in. broad. One end of the column being raised by hydraulic presses a sufficient height—say a foot—it will be kept so raised by a powerful balk of timber slid under it. The other end will then be similarly treated, and thus, slowly but surely, it will ascend foot by foot, shored up with timber at every stage, laid in a way which will best ensure the stability of the whole structure. The jacket, it is thought, will clip the stone sufficiently tight to hold it when in a vertical position; but during the few minutes it will be suspended vertically before being lowered to its base, it will stand in the iron strap as if

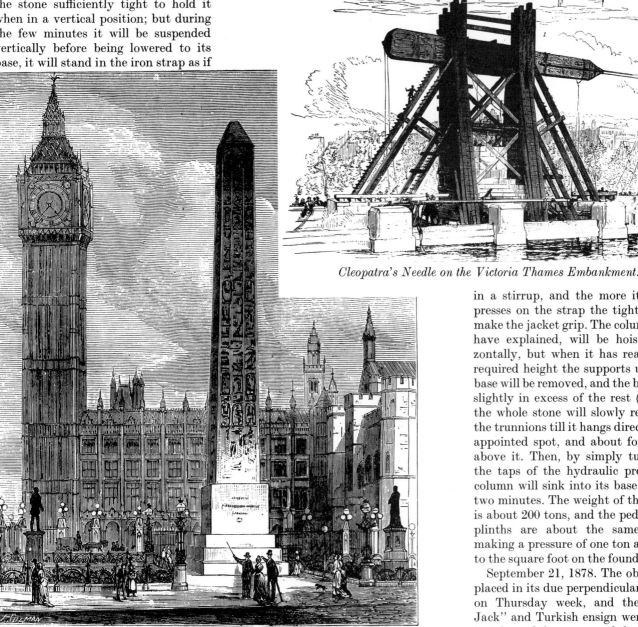

Cleopatra's Needle on the Victoria Thames Embankment.

Wooden Model of the Obelisk on suggested Site in Parliament Square.

in a stirrup, and the more its weight presses on the strap the tighter it will make the jacket grip. The column, as we have explained, will be hoisted horizontally, but when it has reached the required height the supports under the base will be removed, and the base being slightly in excess of the rest ($2\frac{1}{2}$ tons), the whole stone will slowly revolve on the trunnions till it hangs direct over its appointed spot, and about four inches above it. Then, by simply turning on the taps of the hydraulic presses, the column will sink into its base in about two minutes. The weight of the column is about 200 tons, and the pedestal and plinths are about the same weight, making a pressure of one ton and a half to the square foot on the foundations.

September 21, 1878. The obelisk was placed in its due perpendicular attitude on Thursday week, and the "Union Jack" and Turkish ensign were run up in token of the success of the work.

The East Lond

spital for Children, 1872.

The idea of a railway tunnel through the Alps between Fourneaux, near Modane, on the northern side, and Bardonnèche, on the Italian or southern side, has been conceived long before, though it was not till the year 1857 that the excavation was actually commenced, and the special apparatus for using the force of compressed air in boring was not applied till June, 1861 ... The arch of the tunnel is nearly semicircular; it is 25 ft. 3½ in. wide at the base, 26 ft. 2¾ in. at the broadest part, and 24 ft. 7 in. high at the Modane end, but 11¼ in. higher at the Bardonnèche end . . . An iron frame or carriage, travelling along the rails and coming close to the uncut face of the rock, holds some rather complex machinery, which has a two-fold action—namely, that of a piston in a cylinder for propelling the boring tool against the rock; and, secondly, a rotary action which at the same time works the valve of the propelling cylinder and gives a twist to the boring tool when it enters the rock. A second pipe accompanies each borer and pours in a little water to moisten the rock. The whole apparatus com-

Boring Machine in the New Railway Tunnel of the Alps.

municates by a larger flexible hose with the fixed iron tube from which it draws its supply of condensed air. . . . It is expected that the tunnel will be finished three years hence; the total cost of the tunnel and its thirty-four miles of approaches is estimated at between £5,400,000 and £7,200,000.

Completion of the St. Gothard Tunnel: Arrival at Airolo of the first Train coming through the Tunnel, March 1880.

The Elevated Railway, New York.

THE ZULU WAR

[Cetewayo, tyrannical ruler of the Zulu, had disputed the Transvaal borders for some years. When no answer was received to demands for compensation for border raids, a British force invaded Zululand in 1879 under General Lord Chelmsford. A force of over 1,200 British was overwhelmed and slaughtered on January 22: there was a notable and successful defence at Rorkesdrift; and final victory came in July at Ulundi.]

The victory at Ulundi, achieved by the division of our troops under the direct command of Lord Chelmsford, suggests more than one topic of satisfaction to the British public. It gives something approaching definiteness to the previously hazy prospect of bringing the war in Zululand to a speedy conclusion. Cetewayo must now be alive to the fact that, as a belligerent, he is overmatched.

Encampment of the Thames Rowing Club.

87

The Zulu War: Isandhlwana Revisit
From a sketch by our spec

Fetching away the Waggons.

ist Mr. Melton Prior.

The Zulu War: The Fin...
From sketches supplied b...

Repulse of the Zulus at Ginghilovo.
Lieutenant-Colonel J. North Crealock.

His chief Kraal, the centre, we may call it, of his Sovereignty, has been taken and burned to the ground. . .

Another matter for congratulation may be found in the conduct of our troops. On no occasion have they exhibited greater steadiness in action. Young though the great majority of them may be, and therefore unseasoned against panic in the face of visible and appalling danger, they stood their ground with all the coolness and undaunted determination of veteran soldiers . . . But one cannot avoid the inference that, although successful in the instance before us, the immature age at which so considerable a proportion of our fighting army was hurried off to South Africa, cannot be repeated without enormous peril, and reveals some serious defect in our present Army organisation at home.

It would be folly to pretend that this victory at Ulundi is one of a character the recollection of which our country will cherish with a glow of patriotic pride. The war which, it is hoped, it will bring to a close, has never been one in which the people of Great Britain have taken an approving interest. It was initiated without consulting their wishes. The policy of it, however it may please the Cape Colonists, never commended itself to the authorities or to the People of the United Kingdom. It has not been popular even in the Army. The country, having been dragged into it, could not, of course, put an end to the War, in the face of the disasters it had sustained, until it had sufficiently demonstrated its power of ascendancy. This it has now done, and it may be pretty confidently said that the best incident of the Zulu War is that which opens a way out of it.

MR. GLADSTONE AT THE BANQUET IN LEEDS

The truly Yorkshire welcome given by the population of Leeds to the Prime Minister and his family has been unsurpassed for its cordiality, splendour, and completeness. Mr. Gladstone was received with the homage due to the pre-eminent statesman of the nation rather than the leader of a party. The hospitality included a monster banquet in the extemporised hall in the old Cloth-yard, followed by a torch-light procession of some 2,500 working men, who escorted Mr. Gladstone to Headingly. The Prime Minister repaid the enthusiasm of the citizens of Leeds— which lasted without flagging from Thursday to Saturday [October 6–8 1881]—with a series of masterly addresses on the public questions of the day, delivered with unfailing vigour and more than his accustomed impressiveness.

The "fair trade" question was grappled with in one of his earliest speeches: it was not the condition of our foreign trade, but the deficient harvests, which have made us a hundred millions poorer, that lie at the root of the depression of trade . . . The Prime Minister has not shirked the Irish difficulty, and in his address on Friday evening he spoke with the utmost frankness and solemnity on this "burning question". He considers that the passing of the Land Act imposes on the Government new and special obligations with reference to the enforcement of the law and the public peace . . . In the last of his series of speeches he touched and threw considerable light upon the foreign policy of England, and on Indian and colonial affairs. Whether the tone of his addresses be regarded as too highly pitched or not, it cannot be contested that their entire scope tended to elevate public feeling and to subdue party bitterness.

The Fine Art Institution: The Picture Gallery—Old Masters.

A Picnic at Netley Abbey, Southampton.

The War in Egypt: The Battle of Tel-el-Kebir: First in the Fray.

VICTORY IN EGYPT

[Following a military rising against Anglo-French rule in Egypt, led by Arabi Pasha, in the summer of 1882, Sir Garnet Wolseley led a force against the Egyptians and defeated Arabi at the battle of Tel-el-Kebir.]

In a great and decisive battle at Tel-el-Kebir on Tuesday, Sept. 13, Sir Garnet Wolseley, at five o'clock in the morning, with about fifteen thousand troops who had made a night march of six miles from Kassassin, in less than half an hour stormed the fortified position of the Egyptian Army, held by twenty-two thousand men with forty guns, and completely dispersed the enemy's forces, Arabi Pasha taking to flight, and leaving the road open to Zagazig and Cairo. . .

MR. PRIOR'S LECTURE ON THE WAR IN EGYPT

His Royal Highness the Prince of Wales on Wednesday evening, Feb. 21, 1883, paid a visit to the Savage Club at Lancaster House, Savoy, and presided over a most entertaining soirée.

A lecture by Mr. Melton Prior, Special War Artist of *The Illustrated London News* for the past decade, on the War in Egypt, was the first item on the programme. It was listened to with unabated attention throughout; and the vivid battle scenes thrown by the lime-light on the screen presented a most interesting panorama of the naval and military operations of Lord Alcester and Lord Wolseley. It was in a happy, colloquial manner that Mr. Prior at the outset of his lecture told how Mr. William Ingram [editor of *The Illustrated London News*] in the summer of last year dispatched him, almost at a moment's notice, to Egypt in the service of this Journal; and the great value of the cartoons shown in Mr. Prior's lecture on the naval and military operations is that they are nearly all enlarged from the original sketches made by him under fire in Egypt. These were clearly thrown on the screen and each tableau was so bold and effective as to lend

force to the illusion that Mr. Prior was describing the stirring events as they happened before the spectators.

The salient features of the Bombardment—a general view of the Fleet shelling the forts, Bluejackets at their guns, and the battered forts of Arabi—were quickly followed by equally animated tableaux of Alexandria in flames, and Lord Charles Beresford putting

The Royal Pier, Southampton, Summer 1883.

martial law in force against incendiaries. Spirited sketches of the reconnaissances, life-like portraits of Sir Garnet and H.R.H. the Duke of Connaught introduced the advance to Cairo; and the interest was increased as Mr. Prior succintly pointed out the familiar incidents of the Night Charge of Sir Drury Lowe at Kassassin, and the dashing episodes of the capture of Tel-el-Kebir. The Prince of Wales said: "Everybody has known for years that Mr. Melton Prior is a clever Artist; but few probably were aware that he is so graphic a lecturer. I have just been told that this very interesting lecture has lasted an hour; but it seemed to me only ten minutes."

We may add that Mr. Prior is to deliver his Lecture on the War in Egypt for the first time in public at the Crystal Palace on the current Friday afternoon. . .

HENLEY REGATTA

The most attractive and agreeable event of its kind, if the weather be dry and bright, in these days of cheerful June, is the annual contest of amateur rowers on that noble reach of the river Thames between the bridge of Henley and the islet of Remenham. Our Sketches will serve at least to remind those who in past years have enjoyed the pleasant gathering that it had its peculiar delights. There are few places up the river which have a more agreeable reputation; and it is somewhat beyond the range of holiday-making Cockneydom. The banks are here adorned with stately poplars, behind which are the beautiful woods of Park Place, with a curious architectural ornament, General Conway's Druidical temple, removed from Jersey, on the slope of the hill. Below the starting-point of the regatta are several "eyots" or "aits", diminutive islands, overgrown with osiers, and bearing some larger trees, their shores encompassed with rushes and water-loving flowers. Inviting spots may here be found on which to land with one's party of friends, in which there should be at least two charming young ladies, the more the happier, and to unpack the hamper containing pasties or sandwiches, champagne or claret, or whatever is refreshing and tempting to the taste. Boats of various descriptions, with hands that are skilful or those which are clumsy to wield the dipping oars, and steam-launches with commodious saloons, or with small cabins where the sitters are sadly cramped, bring their respective freight of passengers to share the day's amusement. It is a Midsummer festival on the Thames which one would like to see again and again.

(Top of the page) A Poor Weak Mortal. (Above) Towing—A Fair Team.

An aquatic tea party at Brighton.

A swimming class at Brighton.

London Sketches—Regent Circus

...ford Street, during the Season.

The DANDY of pre-historic times

The Ariel of modern times

The 'Bone-shaker' of the middle ages

Under Foll Sail

The police have strict orders to arrest any Bicyclist riding without a bell or whistle

The Bicycle—Some Types observed.

The trial of life-saving apparatus on the Serpentine, Hyde Park.

An experimental trial of the working of marine life-saving appliances took place last week [July, 1883] on the Serpentine, in Hyde Park, under the direction of the Commissioners of the International Fisheries Exhibition. On the south side of the Serpentine, near the bathing place, a short wooden pier was built out in the water, and to this was moored the new lifeboat, *Arab*, which is to be stationed at Padstow, on the north coast of Cornwall. About twenty men of the crew of the Eastbourne lifeboat station, wearing their blue jerseys and red woollen caps, and equipped with cork jackets, were assembled to work the different kinds of floating craft, traps and gear, contributed to the exhibition. A tent was erected for the committee and jurors who were to award the prizes, and there was a fair gathering of spectators, besides some in the boats on the water. The performances began with the lifeboat manoeuvres; and when the crew purposely upset their boat, to show how quickly it would right itself, the spectators were greatly pleased.

They were next called upon to notice Mr. Copeman's invention of an article which is convertible at will from an ordinary deck-seat into a serviceable sea-raft. It has been approved by the Board of Admiralty, and is in use on board the vessels of the Peninsular and Oriental and other first-class steam navigation companies. The raft is formed of a couple of buoyant wooden benches, fitted with spars, mast, sail, oars, water, provisions, and signals. It was quickly launched, and made to sail about as handily and easily as a well-constructed open boat. Rafts were also exhibited by Messrs. J. and A. W. Birts, Mr. Meiter, and Captain Drevar. At one time there were in the water mattresses, pillows, belts, swimming plates, oil-skin dresses, and ship's furniture, all constructed with the object of saving life at sea. Not the least remarkable among these were Mr. Williams's portable pontoons. They consist of a series of oblong iron troughs, which pack one within the other like so many Chinese or Japanese lacquer cups. Mr. Williams claims that ten men can in the space of fifteen minutes fix together and launch twenty rafts capable of accommodating one thousand shipwrecked persons. Messrs. Birts' double mess-table raft was invented with the idea of saving soldiers in troopships for whom there may be no room in the boats, and forms one of a collection of articles which gained the gold medal of the Society of Arts in 1879. Sexton's buoyant deck seats are of ingenious construction, and would prove useful in case of emergency. They can be easily freed from the deck, and, on being loosed, would float out in three parts, each separate and distinct from the rest, and fitted with lockers for stores.

Messrs. Pocock Brothers' cylinder bed, Mr. Holmes's life-preserving mattress, and Mr. Da Sala's canvas boat are all designed with a view to portability and cheapness combined. Nothing could however, be more simple of its kind, or probably more efficacious in the moment of danger, than Captain Cressy's bed-cot frames, made buoyant with cork, and fitted with corrugated wire netting, except in the middle, which has an opening for the body to pass through. The scene on the Serpentine, when the water was covered with all sorts of rafts, canoes, buoys, and swimming gear, men and lads delighting in the fun of such ventures, and all in perfect safety, was very amusing to those on shore.

Fig. 1.

Fig. 2.

Fig. 4.

Fig. 3.

Fig. 5.

Fig. 6.

I.T.BALCOMB del

THE PHONOGRAPH

This is an age of scientific marvels, if not of miracles. To railways and steamboats, making near neighbours of distant provinces and practically bridging oceans, succeeded the electric telegraph, which turned into a verity Puck's boast of girdling the earth in forty minutes; and now we have the phonograph, which machine first imprints a message and then speaks or sings it off any number of times at the operator's will. Persons have only to speak or sing into the mouthpiece of the simple-looking instrument and they may have the pleasure of hearing their own sweet voices reproduced many times.

The phonograph is as simple in construction as it appears, consisting of a cylinder mounted on a horizontal axle, and capable of rotation by a handle, or preferably, as uniformity of speed is essential, by clockwork. The cylinder is not only capable of rotation, but also has a gentle lateral movement. A screw-thread is cut on the cylinder, and the cylinder itself is coated with tinfoil. This tinfoil is gently pressed by a metal pin, or style, which is attached to a thin disc of iron furnished with a funnel-shaped mouthpiece of vulcanite. When words are spoken into the mouthpiece, the vibrations of the air are communicated to the metal diaphragm, and the pin presses against the cylinder

as it travels along . . . The phonograph is the invention of Mr. Thomas Elvey Edison, a well-known electrician, of Menlo Park, New Jersey, United States.

AUTOMATA

At the wonderful exhibition at the "Home of Mystery" in the Egyptian Hall, Piccadilly, Mr. John Nevile Maskelyne and Mr. John Algernon Cooke present four ingenious mechanical figures, apparently self-acting or automatic, which have been admired by thousands of curious and wondering visitors, and the secret of whose motions no one has been able to guess. These are Psycho, the Hindoo whist-player, card-player in general, and arithmetician; Zoe, a pretty little lady in Greek costume, who writes and draws portraits; Fanfare, the cornet-player, and another musician, named Labial, who performs on the euphonium. The figures are too small for even a little boy or girl to be concealed inside them, and they are placed on glass pedestals, which might be supposed to preclude any communication with them by wires, cords, or tubes . . .

New Year's greetings by telephone, January 1882.

The reporters' room in the House of Commons.

The marriage of the Duke of Connaught and Prince

ouise Margaret of Prussia at Windsor, March 1879.

Having been frequently requested to give information to lecturers on Art and others of different processes connected with the publication of *The Graphic*, it has occurred to us that some information on the subject may not be altogether uninteresting to the public.

It is a common remark made to us, "How can you find fresh subjects to fill so many pages week after week?" But so far from there being any difficulty on that score, our greatest trouble is the constant rejection of valuable material for want of room. Thanks, however, to two great factors, we hope to be able to lessen this. The first is the large and constantly increasing support of the public, secondly, the powers of Electricity now called to our aid. Although aspiring to have some influence for good on the advancement of Art, we do not forget we have always been, and wish to continue, a *News* Paper.

Only ten years ago, if an event suitable for pictorial illustration occurred on the Saturday, it was considered sharp work to sketch, draw on the wood, engrave, electrotype, and print the subject to be illustrated for the issue of the following Saturday. By improved machinery it has become possible to illustrate an event happening on the Tuesday of the same week, and now we propose, by the aid of the new electro-dynamo machines, to save many hours in electrotyping, and so be able to give our latest news-pictures up to Wednesday evening.

We propose, therefore, frequently to give with *The Graphic* an extra *sketch sheet*, thus bringing up our news to the latest moment, largely increasing the number of our engravings, and, consequently, rejecting fewer of the many subjects of interest sent us by our kind correspondents.

Gentle reader, before this Christmas Number is laid on one side, let us try and convey to you the amount of trouble, and labour, and anxiety it has caused, and the number of busy hands it has occupied. More than twelve months ago many artists had already placed in our hands their pictures, and

our task is to deliver to you for a shilling faithful copies of works that have cost many thousands of pounds.

First, a picture is photographed on to box-wood, and engraved. This is called the key, or black block. Then has to be produced each colour-plate in relief like the engraved block, only in metal—buff, yellow, pink, brown, blue, crimson, and so on, altogether fourteen colour plates.

School of Engraving.

There are no less than nine separate printings on, say, a child's face, two yellow tints, three flesh, two grey, besides a brown and blue—the effect and gradation required being produced by the action of acid on copper plates, the acid being allowed to bite or eat away the lighter parts, leaving the darks in relief.

Each plate then has an impression taken by a hand press, one on the top of another. The result when finished is appalling, and it would be dangerous to show even the most good-tempered and genial artist the proof. This colour must be altered, that plate thrown away, and another re-done, this colour softened, that strengthened. At last another proof

The Engraving Studio.

Finishing the Electrotypes.

Engraving at Night.

is reprinted, with better result. The fourteen plates are now ready for the machine; but to enable the number to be printed by Christmas (we may now suppose ourselves starting about April) each plate must be duplicated by electrotyping.

The process of electrotyping may be briefly described as follows. The wood block or colour plate is placed in a bed of wax, which has been melted, and allowed to cool until it has arrived at the proper consistency. It is then submitted to a great pressure in a press of hydraulic or other construction, and in this way a *facsimile* of the original is produced, but with every detail reversed. This wax impression is then covered with a thin coating of black lead, such being a good conductor of electricity, and is hung by means of a brass rod in a large bath filled with a solution of sulphate of copper, sulphuric acid, &c. Side by side with this bath is a powerful battery of Smee's construction, that is to say zinc, and platinised silver in dilute sulphuric acid. The current generated by this battery is put into connection with the wax mould hung in the bath, and also with a sheet of copper also hung there side by side with the mould. The effect of the electricity is in the first place to decompose the copper, and in the second place to attract the particles of copper to the mould. In a short time a thin coating of copper has formed upon the mould, of which it is again the reverse, and consequently the exact facsimile of the original block. The shell, as it is called, is then filled up at the back with metal in order to make the surface perfectly hard and suitable for printing, and after being made smooth and uniform in thickness by means of lathes and planing machines, it is mounted upon wood and is ready for the machine.

In place of the battery above mentioned, the current of electricity is now largely obtained from a dynamo-electric machine. It is simply a modification of the machine by which the electric light is produced, and in which the current is obtained by the rapid revolution of a ring of soft iron bound round with coils of wire in front of the poles of a series of powerful magnets.

A machine now starts on its task of printing over half-a-million impressions. One printer has charge of the machine, and is responsible for the excellence of the work. He has under his command two youths who lay on, and one who takes off. The layers-on have to adjust each sheet by pin-holes on to little pins to get the exact register. Here let the reader dismiss any preconceived notions of rattling off thousands per hour, as is ordinarily done with printing from type. Engravings, whether in black or colour, must have a fair time to get a good, clean impression, and the machine has yet to be made that can print well at a speed above eight or nine hundred an hour. The printer has to watch each sheet with the eye of an artist, see that it is printed the proper strength, and throw out any faulty impressions.

At length the impression is taken to another machine, exactly the same routine goes on as for the first colour, again to the third, and so on to the fourteenth.

In the meantime authors and compositors have not been idle; and other machines are now in readiness to receive the sheets of coloured pictures which

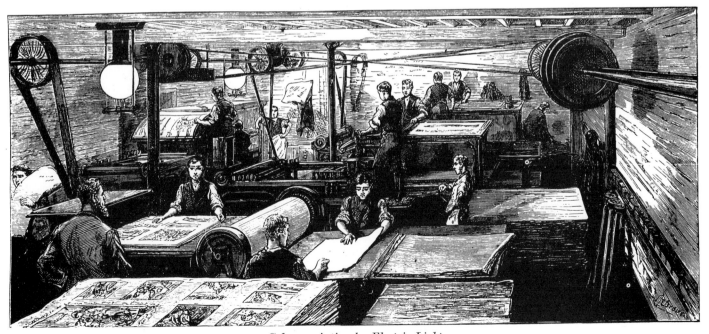

Colour-printing by Electric Light.

require printing at the back. This printing of the letter-press can be done at a quicker speed, and the sheets are then taken to the folding-room.

The folding machine is a dear, winning, fascinating instrument. Though small, it has an enormous appetite, and it is fed on one side by a man with an open sheet of the number, another side by another sheet, and, as if this were not enough, a third man artfully contrives to introduce the cover, or

fault of theirs, they cannot supply.

On the morning of publication—the whole trade having previously paid for the quantities they require—the publishing office is besieged by eager messengers from wholesale houses, and by the retail dealer, anxious for the stroke of the clock announcing the opening of the "list". The roadway and adjacent streets are closely packed with vehicles of every description, from the two-horse van to the common costermonger's bar-

22nd of November, that is if you were to walk twelve hours a day; or, to put the matter in another way, the sheets of paper used by *The Graphic* in one year, if laid side by side, would reach just half round the world.

The Graphic, at its beginning, rented one house, and began to print with six machines. Now there are three large buildings, containing twenty printing machines, invented by our master printer (besides ten machines constantly

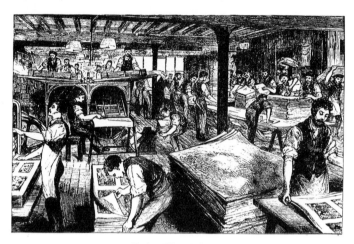

(*Left*) *The Folding Room.* (*Right*) *Printing the ordinary Weekly Issue of* The Graphic.

wrapper. Nothing daunted, the machine snatches at all three, folds them into four or two as wanted, puts each of them into their proper place in the cover, and delivers them as fast as your pulse beats.

The Christmas Number having been printed, packed in quires, and handed over to the publisher, his troubles now

The Store Room.

begin. He has over half-a-million copies, representing a total cost of about Twenty-one Thousand pounds, and he does not quite know whether public favour will leave him with forty or fifty thousand on his hands, or whether the demand will so largely exceed his supply that he will lay himself open to numbers of actions at law and claims for damages (as happened on a former occasion) from exasperated newsagents, who have taken orders which, through no

row, and the services of the police are needed to regulate the traffic without, and to keep in check the more turbulent spirits within. The "list" having been opened, each house is taken in its alphabetical order, and their collectors served, whether it be the modest single quire, or four thousand quires. Hastening with their burdens at full speed to their respective offices, all is hurry and bustle to catch the first train with the parcels, which they in turn distribute to their country customers, and they again to the public, every one's anxiety being to be first. As our American cousins display the same impatience, arrangements are now made by which *The Graphic* Christmas Number is published at the same hour in both England and *in every American State*, and most of the Colonies. Thus the continuous labour of nearly twelve months is dispersed in a few hours, and we begin to think of *next* Christmas.

A few plain figures may be considered interesting. Counting artists, authors, papermakers, printers, &c., we calculate that *The Graphic* employs about a thousand people, that the annual outlay is over one hundred and twenty thousand pounds, the weight of paper used a thousand tons, and if you were to lay it down, in sheets, and walk on it, at the rate of three miles an hour, and start on Christmas day, you would come to the end of your *Graphic* walk on the

employed by us outside), illuminated with the electric light by the Metropolitan Brush Company's lamps of 2,000 candle power (nominal), worked by means of a dynamo-machine on their premises near the Victoria Embankment. There are also telephonic communication with four departments, another building devoted to electrotyping and stereotyping, and one now in course of erection to contain the new dynamo-electric machine, and two more printing machines driven by gas engines [1882].

Publishing the Christmas Number.

— The Start —

Throwing out Papers

Folding-Van

Guard's Van

The Arrival — Scramble for Papers

Notes on an early newspaper train.

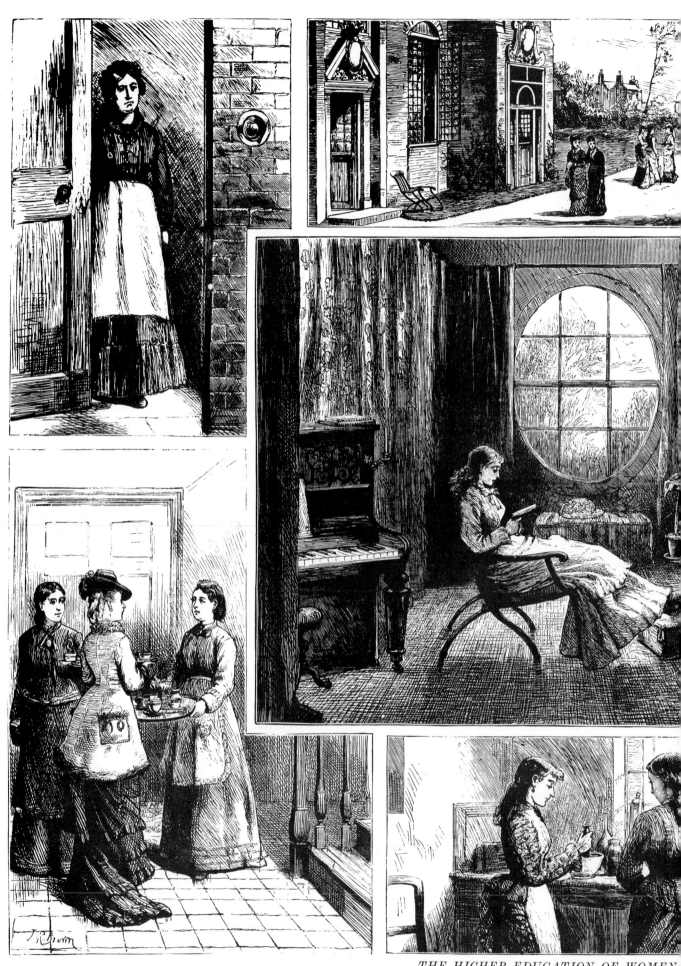

THE HIGHER EDUCATION OF WOMEN—
1. The Portress. 2. The Terrace, Newnham Hall. 3. A Study. 4. A Lectur

HE LADIES' COLLEGES AT CAMBRIDGE.
irton College. 5. An Afternoon Cup. 6. The Laboratory. 7. The Dining Hall.

The fees in the London Board Schools range from a penny to ninepence a week. There is no free Board School in the metropolis, nor indeed anywhere in England and Wales. The Board has power under the Act of Parliament to "remit" or forgo the fees in case of poverty. The aggregate amount of fees collected in a year is about 120,000*l.*, and the remission of fees amounts to little short of 10,000*l.* a year, while a very large sum in the shape of irrecoverable arrears is annually struck off the accounts.

Children are received into the schools for instruction at three years of age. At the age of seven they pass out of the infants' department into the boys' or girls' department. After the first course of infant instruction they enter Standard I. The Standards are seven in number. In order to pass the examination in the First Standard the child must read, to the satisfaction of H.M. Inspector, "a short paragraph from a book, not confined to words of one syllable." He must "copy in manuscript characters a line of print, and write from dictation not more than ten easy words, commencing with capital let-ters;" in Arithmetic he is tested in notation and numeration up to 1,000; in simple addition and subtraction of numbers of not more than three figures; not more than five lines to be given in addition; and in the multiplication table up to six times twelve. Some conception may be formed of the work by com-paring this with what is demanded of the child in passing the Seventh Standard:—

"To read a passage from Shakespeare or Milton, or from some other standard author, or from a history of England.

"A theme or letter, Composition, spel-ling, and handwriting to be considered.

"Note books and exercise books to be shown.

"Compound proportion, averages, and percentages."

But the Sixth Standard is the Standard on passing which the child between the ages of ten and thirteen is exempted from compulsory attendance at school; and the child over ten years of age may be at work half time and at school half time on passing in the Third Standard, if the parent satisfies the Boards that, in consequence of poverty, the child's earnings are neces-sary and the employment is beneficial.

The great majority of the teachers in Public Elementary Schools come by a sort of process of natural selection from the ranks of the children who attend these schools. Promising young scholars are drafted into the profession. They begin, at not less than thirteen years of age, as candidates on probation. The candidates must have passed an exam-ination in Standard V or Standard VI, and in two of the class subjects. At the end of the year of probation they must pass in Standard VI or Standard VII, and in two class subjects. They then enter upon a period of apprenticeship to the School Board, and are pupil-teachers; they have to pass an exam-ination at the end of each year of apprenticeship.

Recently the London Board has established pupil-teachers' instruction centres, where the young apprentices are gathered together into classes and specially taught. Upon this plan, in-stead of being required to compress almost the whole of their study and instruction into the time when the children's work is done, they are at work among the children for only one half the time during which the school is open, the remaining half going to swell

A nursery, Great Wild Street.

the time devoted solely to their own preparation. This new scheme is a subject of considerable controversy. There seems to be no question as to its excellent effect upon the pupil-teachers themselves; but the objection is urged that, the money having been spent upon their instruction out of the School Board funds, the pupil-teacher, upon completing his training, is at liberty to accept an engagement in any part of the world. . . The system has not yet been long enough in operation to enable an accurate estimate to be formed of its results. Against its cost there is to be set off a substantial reduction in the

Reading class, Clare Market.

Kindergarten—Plaiting class.

salaries given to pupil-teachers during their apprenticeship, in consideration of the superior education which they now receive. The present payment in the time of apprenticeship is from 5s. a week for boys and 3s. a week for girls in the first year, to 16s. and 10s. in the fourth.

The rate of salary for assistant teachers begins at 50*l.* a year for men and 45*l.* for women, and runs up to 155*l.* respectively. For head teachers the rate ranges from 150*l.* for men and 120*l.* for women to 400*l.* and 300*l.* respectively.

The Board Schools of London are generally very large, accommodating frequently from 1,200 to 1,600 children. Such schools require men of great ability, with exceptional power of organisation and of personal command. It is the opinion of very competent authorities that some of the best head teachers in the world are in the service of the London School Board.

Wonderful is the change wrought in poor and outcast neighbourhoods by the work and influence of the schools. Children who came at first into the new

school dirty, ragged, and wild, soon appear clean and decent, and somehow the poorest parents after a while appear to rise to the conditions, and find the means to make the little folks more presentable.

Kindergarten—Threading beads.

The teaching of the blind is an exceedingly interesting branch of the work. One of the largest blind centres is a special department of the Bowling Green Lane Schools, in Clerkenwell. The headmistress is herself blind; and much of the teaching is done by blind teachers. In oral lessons the children mix with the ordinary class. They sit side by side with the other children in the Government examinations, and pass almost as readily.

There are seven centres for the instruction of deaf and dumb children. One of the largest is in Winchester Street, Pentonville. It is all on the famous lip-reading principle. The teacher gets attention by stamping the foot, which seems effective even in cases of total deafness, the vibration reaching the consciousness of the child otherwise than through the aural organ. The spectacle is very interesting and

Blind class, Shadwell.

articulation to the words. The pupil cannot hear the sounds which he makes and has never heard syllables uttered. This is the great difficulty; but it is in time largely overcome. First the poor students make themselves intelligible to the initiated, and afterwards with some difficulty to the stranger. They enjoy the work immensely, and if it takes a long time to learn to speak without hearing in an absolutely silent world, the children are quick enough in learning to write. They will take soundless dictation from the lips of the teacher, and write down the sentence, or work out the sum, in an almost beautiful hand.

The nursery in Great Wild Street is another of the many affecting sights with the Board Schools in every department present. This is carried on with our expense through the generosity of the widow of the late Lord Stanley of Alderley. The purpose of the nursery is to remove a hardship, often incident upon compulsory school attendance, by taking care of the babies of poor

peculiar. The children are very deft in reading words and sentences from the lips of the teacher; but the trouble is in the use of the voice in giving sound and

(Top of the page) Cleaning up—9 a.m. (Above) Cookery class, Marlborough Road.

Girls' drill, Marlborough Road.

The penny dinner centres are now, at the edge of winter, getting into full and extended operation. There is evidence that this movement is really accomplishing something in furtherance of its objects, in the fact that with the advent of hard times and want of work the number of the diners increases, to fall again with the coming of more prosperous times.

In neighbourhoods the most deplorable, destitute, and forlorn, in schools full of hapless wastrels, the poor child-

families whilst the elder children are attending school. A kind, motherly woman is employed to devote her time to the care and amusement of the little ones, who, under her charge in the warm, bright, toy-strewn room, appear as happy as children could possibly be.

In the Board School cookery class our artist has chosen to sketch, the young girls—as in all the other centres—show the greatest interest in learning how cheap some good dinners may be made, and the teacher's method is admirable without qualification.

Again, in the infants' schools, the bright happiness of the children engaged in the various occupations of the Kindergarten is the first thing that strikes the visitor. Their best intelligence seems to be brought out, without the least suggestion of toil or weariness.

Our artist's picture of a reading class in a Board School by Clare Market gives a glimpse of School Board teaching in the midst of one of the poorest and most densely populated districts in West-Central London. This is one of the schools acknowledged in official lists to be a "school of special difficulty." It is hard and up-hill work for teachers here, but the higher influences of education are clearly and hopefully visible.

Scullery work—Washing up.

Swedish exercise at Limehouse.

ren, especially the younger ones and the girls, evidently find a peculiar interest and pleasure in their work. Labouring in the midst of depressing influences the teachers are found full of zeal and enthusiasm. All this makes a stupendous enterprise, which cannot be summed up in a few words.

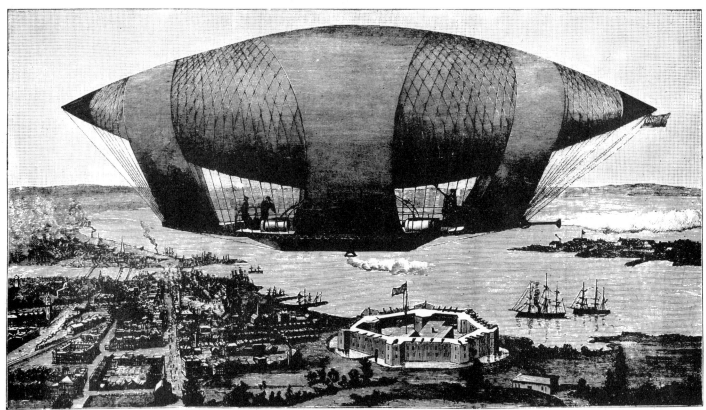

A new navigable American war balloon, motivated by compressed air.

THE CHOLERA IN EUROPE

Those persons whom business takes to the infected districts of Southern France —few are likely to resort thither for pleasure at the present time—will be glad to learn that the fumigation system at the Marseilles and Toulon railway stations has been abolished as useless and vexatious. This disagreeable ordeal was in full force at Avignon early in the month, as is shown in this sketch by Mr. E. Prioleau Warren, A.R.I.B.A., who, with other unfortunates, was exposed for a quarter of an hour to the fumes of strong carbolic acid.

116

[Gordon had been governor of the equatorial provinces 1874–79 and had tried to suppress the slave trade and bring a just and considerate government to the Sudan, which had for years been plagued by venal and corrupt administrations. But after Gordon left the Sudan, the abuses recurred under the Mahdis; and in 1883 an army of more than 10,000 men under Colonel William Hicks was annihilated when the Mahdi took over Kordofan and Sennar. General Gordon was sent to Khartoum to try to enforce the withdrawal of the Mahdi forces in February 1884; but after initial successes for the British, on January 26, 1885, Khartoum was captured by the Mahdi, Gordon killed, and the British expedition withdrawn.]

December 1, 1883. Last week's news of the destruction by hostile Bedouins of Captain Moncrieff and his detachment of troops that had landed at Souakim was only the prelude to a more terrible catastrophe, the consequences of which are likely to be momentous and far-reaching. Of the complete overthrow of the small army led by Hicks Pasha across the deserts of the Soudan to put down the rebellion of the Mahdi, there is, we fear, no doubt. For three days the Egyptians, estimated at 10,000 men, under the command of English officers, fought bravely against overwhelming numbers, but their squares were at length broken, and, as is customary with Orientals, the defeat became a rout. It is a pitiful story. For thirty days, with the scantest supply of water, the expedition had been marching amid great privations, with the alternative of a dear-bought victory or annihilation. Its gallant leaders, whom criminal neglect had left without a base or line of retreat, advanced with a presentiment of their doom. Ammunition, as well as water, failed the Egyptian army which had penetrated to El Obeid. In the last despairing charge against the Mahdi's host the gallant General Hicks appears to have met a soldier's death. His body has been found—one hand grasping a sword, the other a revolver. Fugitives have reported that the entire army was massacred; but there is reason to hope that some were carried into captivity and their lives spared. There is less doubt of the material results of this disastrous campaign. The great province of Soudan, and the equatorial region beyond, are well nigh lost to Egypt, and the Khedive has no available resources adequate to recover them.

The first effect of this disaster has been to arrest the departure of the

In the Soudan—A Letter Home.

British force from Cairo, with a view to protecting Europeans, and to be prepared for all eventualities. The crisis is a serious one. Khartoum, says Sir Samuel Baker—who, next to General Gordon, has the greatest practical acquaintance with the region south of Upper Egypt—must be held at all costs, and he thinks that Soudan may be recovered without much fighting by vigorous measures and prompt concessions to the Abyssinians. Much will, however, depend upon the Mahdi himself. His speedy advance northwards at the head of his victorious host may frustrate all plans carefully prepared at Cairo. His claims as a pseudo-Messiah are calculated to excite the religious fanaticism of the various desert tribes along the banks of the Nile, if they do not attract the sympathy of the Khedive's subjects, and stir up the

Mohammedans of Tripoli and on the borders of Tunis. Like many Pretenders before him Mahomet Achmet professes to be a descendant of the Prophet; and his pretensions will be judged by Moslems, not according to their apparent validity, but by his success as a military leader.

February 9, 1884. Another terrible military disaster, which seems fatal to the last remaining expectation of any recovery of Egyptian dominion in the Soudan, has this week befallen the small remnant of the Khedive's army. General Baker Pasha was utterly defeated last Monday and put to flight with the slaughter of half his troops, in an attempted advance from Trinkitat, on the Red Sea coast, south of Souakim, to relieve the besieged Egyptian garrison of Tokar. The fatal conflict took place near the Wells of Teb, seven miles from Trinkitat, early in the forenoon. We proceed to quote the narrative telegraphed by the *Standard* correspondent:

"The enemy now gathered thickly and advanced towards us, and at nine o'clock showed in considerable force on some slightly rising ground, near the water springs, while on our left front I could see clumps of spears with bannerets partially concealed amidst the hillocks and bushes. Our guns again opened fire; but the shell seemed to pass over the enemy's heads. . .

"Just before this, I had ridden along by the infantry column, and I saw that it was advancing in the most disorderly manner. There was no sign of discipline or steadiness; it was a mere armed mob tramping along. I was convinced they would break at the first charge. As the cavalry rode wildly in, the order was given for the infantry to form square—a manoeuvre in which they had been daily drilled for weeks. At this crisis, however, the dull, half-disciplined mass failed to accomplish it. Three sides were formed after a fashion, but on the fourth side two companies of the Alexandria Regiment, seeing the enemy coming on leaping and brandishing their spears,

stood like a panic-stricken flock of sheep, and nothing could get them to move into their place. Into the gap thus left in the square the enemy poured, and at once all became panic and confusion. The troops fired indeed, but for the most part straight into the air. The miserable Egyptian soldiers refused even to defend themselves, but throwing away their rifles, flung themselves on the ground and grovelled there, screaming for mercy. No mercy was given, the Arab spearmen pouncing upon them and driving their spears through their necks or bodies. Nothing could surpass the wild confusion, camels and guns mixed up together, soldiers firing into the air, with wild Arabs, their long hair streaming behind them, darting among them, hacking and thrusting with their spears.

"While the charge had been made by the enemy on the left flank, General Baker with his Staff were out with the cavalry in front. Upon riding back they found that the enemy had already got between them and the column. . . When the General finally reached the square, the enemy had already broken it up, and it was clear that all was lost."

General Gordon arrived at Korosko last Saturday, and started thence on his

journey across the Desert; he expected to reach Berber in five days, on his way to Khartoum.

February 16, 1884. General Gordon is no longer a lone man crossing the trackless desert. He has reached Berber, and found everything favourable to his purpose, and he is in no way dismayed by the distressful news from the East coast. The tribes around are friendly, and his moral supremacy over the Soudanese appears to be undiminished. "The people," he says, "are coming in to meet me on all sides with enthusiasm." His journey up the Nile to Khartoum is not without its dangers, but General Gordon is confident of success in providing for the retreat of the garrison, and in arranging to give back to the native chiefs "the ancestral power" which had been usurped by Egypt.

March 1, 1884. The surrender of Tokar, its garrison not caring to wait for the relief promised by the British military expedition, was made known in London yesterday week. These men could easily and safely have held out for some time longer, having provisions to the end of the month and great store of ammunition; but they were not inclined to fight. . . . The reports from Khartoum

Defending the square.

Death of a gallant officer in the Soudan.

and the interior of the Soudan are satisfactory. General Gordon is going on well with his work of pacific arrangement. The town is quiet, and the Arabs are freely bringing into the market food and other country produce. All the Egyptian troops have been removed out of the town, in readiness for their long journey down the Nile to Egypt. . .

March 15, 1884. When Her Majesty's Ministers peremptorily required the Egyptian Government to withdraw their garrisons from the Soudan, they probably had little idea of the complications at home and abroad that would ensue. The force of events is tending to change their motto "Rescue and Retire," into "Rescue and Remain". It is thwarting the plans, and paralysing the arm of General Gordon himself. For the moment, that unrivalled master of Oriental diplomacy is bewildered. He has already painful evidence that his withdrawal from Khartoum would consign the vast region around to anarchy and tribal conflicts, and in his desperation—as we must suppose—he is said to have suggested that there is only one man capable of bringing order out of chaos in the Soudan. Zebehr Pasha, at present in exile in Cairo, would no doubt, as Sultan of Khartoum, rule that

province with a rod of iron. But the idea of setting up the King of the Slave-traders, and the "Scourge of Central Africa," as an irresponsible despot over the Arabs of the Soudan is naturally repugnant to English opinion, and it is satisfactory to know that the Government at home have virtually vetoed the appointment. . . Before telegraphic communication with Khartoum is entirely severed—and it is already interrupted—it is to be hoped that the Government will have instructed General Gordon to remain indefinitely in the capital of the Soudan, and exercise supreme authority at his own discretion.

March 22, 1884. General Gordon's movements are still shrouded in mystery. Before the telegraph wire was cut more than a week ago, he was apprehensive of being shut up in Khartoum by a chief who represents the interests of the Mahdi on the banks of the Nile between that city and Berber, and who is preparing to attack Shendy. Our Government have finally declined to put that part of the Soudan under the rule of Zebehr Pasha, but it does not appear that they have persuaded General Gordon to remain at Khartoum as dictator. It is to be hoped that no

more military expeditions in Eastern Soudan will be found necessary, and that General Gordon's ready resource may eventually triumph over the perils that beset him in Khartoum. But we are told that his position is exciting increased uneasiness in official circles at Cairo.

May 3, 1884. Amid the maze of contradictory reports which are telegraphed from Cairo, it has become manifest that Berber is past all relief, and that General Gordon is shut out from all communication with the capital of Egypt. . . His Egyptians are as unreliable as those who surrendered at Tokar. They may, however, be able, behind fortifications, to exhibit a courage which fails them in the field. If they are to be trusted, our noble representative and his companions are safe behind the strong defences of Khartoum. But it is useless to disguise that he is quite beyond the reach of help from Egypt.

June 28, 1884. Amid the contradictory reports that are telegraphed from Cairo, it is clear that the Mahdi himself has not stirred from El Obeid and General Gordon manfully holds his own at Khartoum. . .

September 6, 1884. General Lord Wolseley, who again takes immediate

The Royal Procession passing alo

Castle-street, Liverpool, May 1886.

command of the British forces in Egypt, and who will personally command the expedition up the Nile, to Dongola and probably to Khartoum, for the relief of General Gordon and the military evacuation of the Soudan, left England at the end of last week...

November 15, 1884. There is very little news this week of positive importance with regard to Lord Wolseley's expedition. The Commander-in-Chief is at Dongola, with the advanced portion of his force, while the tedious work of bringing up the remainder is being performed as well as circumstances permit... No additional intelligence of General Gordon's situation at Khartoum has been received...

January 10, 1885. A letter has been received from General Gordon, dated Dec. 14, in which he simply says "All right at Khartoum"; it was written on a scrap of paper the size of a postage stamp...

January 17, 1885. There is good cause to hope that the advanced force of Lord Wolseley's army will have reached that of General Gordon on the Nile below Khartoum by the end of the present week...

February 14, 1885. A painful revulsion

The Prince and Princess of Wales opening the Institute for Working Lads, Whitechapel, November 1, 1885.

of feeling was caused by the news published on Thursday morning that Khartoum, instead of being "relieved" by the gallant advance of Sir Herbert Stewart's brigade, had fallen into the hands of the Mahdi, its Egyptian garri-

The Prince of Wales in the slums of Dublin—Poor children trying to shake hands with His Royal Highness.

son having surrendered, apparently, on Tuesday, Jan. 27. Different versions of the tragedy are received at British headquarters; one story is that General Gordon was not shot, but was killed with swords and spears. The soldiers had consulted among themselves whether to take him alive or not, but they decided upon killing him, "because if they took him alive to the Mahdi he would be spared, and they did not wish this, as they thought he ought to be killed, as he was the cause of all the trouble."

UNDER CANVAS AT BOWDON

Camp of Manchester Working Lads at Bowdon, Cheshire.
1. General View of the Camp. 2. "Lights Out!" 3. A Corner of the Kitchen. 4. A Morning Dip.

Last year a number of the lads belonging to the Hulme and Chorlton-on-Medlock Lads' Club, situated in Mulberry Street, Hulme, were taken to Strines, in Derbyshire, to spend a few days under canvas. The experiment was so successful, and gave such pleasure to the lads, that it was determined to repeat it this year during Whit-week, which is always a period of holiday-making in Lancashire. The programme was as follows:—A camp was formed on the ground of the shooting range at Bowdon, Cheshire, which was kindly lent for the occasion. Tents were erected for sleeping, kitchens for cooking food, and a canteen and large mess tent were provided for use in the evenings. Each day the lads were to undergo a short drill and, for the sake of discipline, the routine of a regular military camp was preserved. The amusements provided consisted of cricket and football matches, swimming and bathing, athletic sports, and, in the evenings, concerts and entertainments. There were five hundred applicants for the trip, but the resources of the committee were insufficient to take more than 180. The camp, which is the rifle range of the Third Cheshire Volunteers, is situated on the banks of the Bollin, not far from New Bridge Hollow, on the old Roman road to Chester. It lies in a sheltered position amid undulating ground. Some twenty conical-shaped tents were provided, with wooden floors, each accommodating some ten lads. Besides these, there were the officials' quarters, a large marquee for a mess-room, and a wooden structure for a kitchen. The cooking operations were carried on over trench-fires in the open air.

Mr. Alexander Devine, the originator of the scheme, found the lads wonderfully amenable to discipline. The *reveille* sounded at six A.M., when the boys turned out and washed. Then the morning parade was held. Breakfast followed, both it and the subsequent meals being announced by bugle-call. Lads who were belated were punished by being sentenced to "potato-drill," that is, to peel the potatoes for their own and their companions' dinners. From the *reveille* until "lights out" was sounded at ten P.M., the bulk of the time was the lads' own. It was a great pleasure to see so many lads, some of whom are from almost the lowest class, and who, but a short time ago, were spending their leisure hours in the streets, now enjoying the liberty of country fields, and fast becoming tanned with fresh air and sunshine.

General View of Trafalgar Square during the Meetings of the Unemployed and the Social Democrats.

"Here they come!" The Mob in St. James's Street.

1. Busily employed—A scene in the Strand. 2. A slight political disagreement at Trafalgar Square.

The peace of the metropolis has been disturbed this week [February 13, 1886] and property destroyed and plundered in a manner and to an extent unprecedented in the annals of Modern London. A great demonstration of the unemployed in Trafalgar Square on Monday was made use of by the leaders of the Revolutionary Social and Democratic Federation to repeat some of their recent and most violent denunciations of the propertied classes and of the existing organisation of society; and practical effect was given to their inflammatory harangues by a mob of roughs and ruffians to whom the demonstration afforded an excuse for assembling. An hour before the procession of the unemployed, timed for 3 P.M., arrived in Trafalgar Square, which, and its approaches, became crowded by a vast multitude of on-lookers, estimated at from 15,000 to 20,000 in number, the Social Democrat leaders had appeared on the scene with a red flag, ultimately taking up their position on the raised roadway in front of the National Gallery; while three improvised platforms close to the Nelson Column were occupied by the organisers and orators of the legitimate demonstration of the day. The latter supported a resolution in favour of providing the unemployed with remunerative labour on useful public works, and of proposals of a Fair Trade tendency.

Fair traders, capitalists, Ministerialists, Conservatives were denounced with impartial vehemence by the Social Democratic orators at the north end of the square, prominent among them being Mr. Burns, who unsuccessfully contested Nottingham at the General Election, and the notorious Mr. Hyndman, the former declaring that at their next meeting the bakers' shops at the West End would be sacked. After a good deal of this incendiary speech-making, a large body of roughs, with the Social Democratic leaders, made, about four o'clock, for Pall Mall, where they smashed the windows of the Carlton Club, and, encouraged by their own numbers and the paucity of the policemen to be seen on their route, they smashed right and left the windows of the club-houses in St. James's Street, up which they wended, turning into Piccadilly on their way to Hyde Park. By this time probably some 2,000 strong, they began to indulge their predatory instincts, and diversified their smashing of windows and hurling of missiles at the inmates of passing carriages, by stopping these, dragging from them their lady occupants to be robbed of their ornaments, and by looting several shops, notably a jeweller's and a wine and spirit shop, of which the contents were specially congenial. In Hyde Park they halted to hear a few speeches from their leaders ostensibly in deprecation of their proceedings, but so little effective in restraining them that, on making their way to South Audley Street, smashing the windows along the line of route, they attacked and plundered almost every shop in it—jeweller's, drapers', butchers', poulterers', grocers'—using as missiles such heavy articles as they

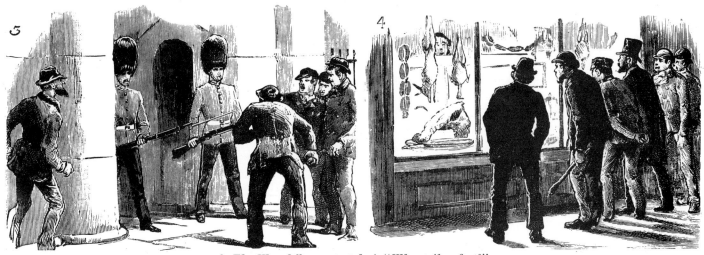

3. The War Office protected. 4. "Who strikes first?"

did not care to carry away with them, and altogether comporting themselves like infuriated savages, the frightened shopkeepers seldom venturing to offer any resistance. Proceeding through Grosvenor Square to North Audley Street, they plundered right and left, and, reaching Oxford Street, stormed and looted the establishments of several jewellers. Meanwhile, however, a body of police had been collected strong enough to confront them at Marylebone Lane, and to prevent much further depredation in the Oxford Street shopkeepers as yet unassailed hastily closed their premises. Then the ruffianly mob gradually melted away, leaving behind them memories of brutal violence and infamous rapine which will not easily be effaced.

Applicants for relief from the Poor Box.

REPORT FROM THE THAMES POLICE COURT

The Thames Police Court is situated in East Arbour Street, Stepney. It is a busy place, to match the busy neighbourhood in which it is located, and drives a more thriving trade in cases of assault and battery, of robbery with violence, of hocussing and garotting, of attempted murder, of actual murder, and the culprit caught red-handed sometimes, than probably any other Court in the metropolis. "Trade" is never slack at the Thames Police Court.

There is no doubt that the prisoners are sure of fair play, and an attentive hearing to their side of the argument.

Entrance to the women's cell.

After a few hours' study of this court, with Mr. Saunders "in the chair", we feel that, were it our ill fate to be "run in" for being drunk and disorderly in the neighbourhood of Stepney, an acute, discriminating, and merciful magistrate would dispense the law with even hand, if not strain it a little in our favour, it being our first offence, say, and it being made perfectly clear to his magisterial mind that we should not do so any more, and were particularly sorry and ashamed to find ourselves in so ignominious a position.

Why, even one Margaret Cain only got a week at this court on the 11th of last January for being drunk and disorderly for the two hundred and twentieth time! She had been doubtful of results, and was apparently grateful for her sentence: "Thank you, and good luck to you" were her farewell words before she was conducted out of Court.

There was great trouble about Lizzie on the morning of our visit to the Thames Police Court, and Lizzie, a general servant "of attractive appearance," as the reporters say—who had appropriated her mistress's brooch for the purpose of personal adornment when she went for a walk on Sunday with her sweetheart—was overwhelmed with grief and remorse, and kept her hands before her face, and sobbed, and choked and gurgled, and became incomprehensible and incoherent in her hysterical defence, and had to be taken in hand by the head gaoler, and talked to in a fatherly manner. But Lizzie only shed copious tears over the gaoler, and sobbed forth that she was dreadfully sorry, and did not take the brooch to sell, and simply borrowed it for a time, and Lizzie being only sixteen, and Lizzie's mother being sponsor for her daughter's future good behaviour, was let off, mercifully and wisely, with a reprimand. Which meant for Lizzie that if she kept strictly to her own finery, and let her mistress's alone, and walked in the ways of honesty from that time forth, nothing more would be heard in the Thames Police Court of her small transgression. . .

Inauguration of Bartholdi's huge Statue of Liberty at New York.

THE NEW YORK STATUE OF LIBERTY

American political independence was much indebted for its victory, a century ago, to French military aid. This was repaid, a very few years later, by the ideas of the American Republic in the great French Revolution. Now that France is again Republican, her sons devoted to that political faith, prompted in 1876, at a centenary festival, by the late M. Laboulaye, an enthusiastic student of the examples of Franklin and Washington, and the translator of Channing, have presented to America, in token of international friendship, a grand artistic gift. M. Bartholdi, the sculptor, by the labour of ten years, constructed at Paris a bronze statue, 151 ft. high, partly at the cost of a public subscription, partly of the French Government. It has been carried across the Atlantic, and has been erected on a small rocky island at the entrance to New York harbour, where it rises 305 ft. above the sea. The figure of crowned "Liberty", uplifting a torch of beneficent light, will henceforth greet the eyes of emigrants and travellers from Europe. The President of the United States, Mr. Grover Cleveland, with his Cabinet Ministers and some members of Congress, received this noble gift and unveiled the statue with due ceremony, on the 28th inst. [November, 1886] in the sight of hundreds of thousands of people.

Life in the Broadwa

New York.

SHOOTING A MAN-EATING CROCODILE

Crocodiles abound in Ceylon, and in many places the natives will "salaam" in dread to the water. At Galle, in the southern province, a saurian was lately killed, whose stomach was found to contain two human skulls. The crocodiles are very wary, and difficult to kill, and generally manage to sink themselves out of sight.

Our sketch is by Major-General H.G. Robley, who writes:— "It is tedious work waiting for the man-eater to come out of the water, but a fat native child as a lure will make the monster speedily walk out of his aqueous lair. Contracting the loan of a chubby infant, however, is a matter of some negotiation, and it is perhaps not to be wondered at that mammas occasionally object to their offspring being pegged down as food for a great crocodile; but there are always some parents to be found whose confidence in the skill of the British sportsman is unlimited. My sketch gives a view of the collapse of the man-eater, who, after viewing the tempting morsel tethered carefully to a bamboo near the water's edge, makes a rush through the sedges. The sportsman, hidden behind a bed of reeds, then fires, the bullet penetrates the heart, and the monster is

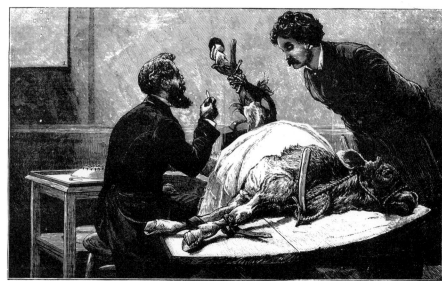

VACCINATION FROM THE CALF: Taking lymph from the calf.

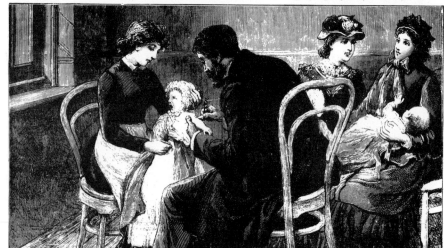

VACCINATION FROM THE CALF: Vaccinating infants.

Sport in Ceylon—Shooting a Man-Eating Crocodile. The Man-Eater's Quietus.

dead in a moment. The little bait, whose only alarm has been caused by the report of the rifle, is now taken home by its doting mother for its matutinal banana. The natives wait to get the musky flesh of the animal, and the sportsman secures the scaly skin and the massive head of porous bone as a trophy."

THE JUBILEE OF HER MAJESTY QUEEN VICTORIA

The Jubilee of Her Majesty the Queen. The Fête for London School Children in Hyde Park.

The celebration on June 21 [1887], of the fiftieth anniversary of the accession of Queen Victoria to the throne of Great Britain and Ireland was for the Queen herself, for the Court and the Royal Family, a solemn religious service of thanksgiving, performed in Westminster Abbey. This mode of expressing both gratitude for the general prosperity of her Majesty's reign, and a sense of dependence on the Divine Will for the continued welfare of the nation, was adopted by many of her subjects who on Tuesday attended special worship in their churches or chapels. To the more numerous portion of our fellow-countrymen, the day was one simply of an appointed public festival, commemorating a happy event, and appealing to the feelings of personal esteem and

good-will commonly entertained for the Queen and the Royal Family, as well as to the recognition of those political and social benefits, and that remarkable growth of the kingdom and empire, which have been obtained in the past fifty years.

In one way or another, the great majority of the English people have shared in this celebration. All over England, Wales, and Scotland, local efforts to make it worthily conspicuous and notable have been zealously promoted. London, as the metropolis, was especially bound, upon this occasion, in the presence of the Queen herself, of all the Princes and Princesses, and of an extraordinary gathering of visitors from different parts of Europe, to give expression to the national sentiment of

loyalty. The sincerity and cordiality with which Londoners of all classes have entered into the purpose of this Jubilee cannot be mistaken. They did not merely stare at the banners, emblems, and mottoes displayed in the streets, as a gay and pretty show, but comments were overheard in the crowd that bespoke a lively sense of patriotic pride and honest friendship to the Royal family—not profoundly reverent, or ardently enthusiastic, but manifestly the outcome of sound popular opinion.

The children's fete for the 30,000 little ones, drawn from the various London Schools took place in Hyde Park on the afternoon of Wednesday, the 22nd of June, and passed off without any

The Jubilee of Her Majesty the Queen—Arrival

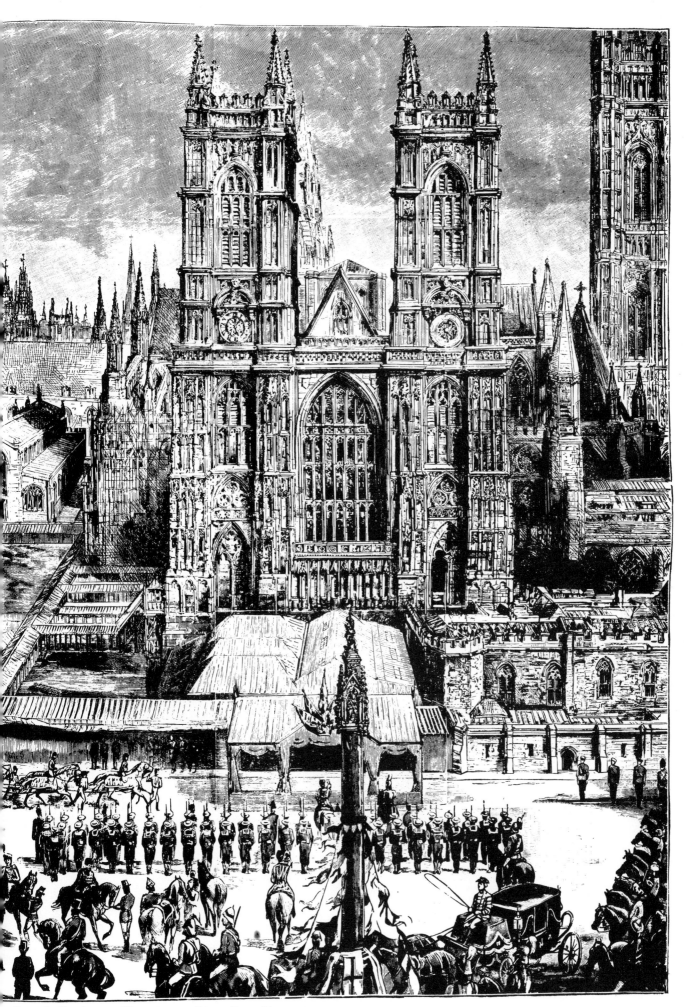

The Queen's Carriage at Westminster Abbey, June 21.

accident to mar its complete success. Refreshments and various amusements were provided for the children. The rations for each child were distributed in paper bags, and consisted of substantial fare, such as meat-pies, squares of cake, and buns, besides oranges; while lemonade, ginger-beer, and milk were supplied as required in each tent. About twenty Punch and Judy entertainments were placed in different parts of the enclosure, besides eight marionette theatres, eighty-six cosmoramic views and peep-shows, nine troupes of performing dogs, monkeys, and ponies, hundreds of 'Aunt Sallies' and 'knock-emdowns', and 100 large lucky-dip barrels. Besides this there were distributed 1,000 skipping-ropes, 10,000 small gas-balloons, and no fewer than 42,000 prizes, consisting of an infinite variety of toys. Medals, moreover, were furnished to the children, having on one side a portrait of the Queen in 1837, and on the other her portrait in 1887. The girls and boys entered into the amusements provided for them with immense zest, and throughout the bright summer afternoon the green sward of the Park was transformed into an admirable playground, where the children disported themselves to their boundless satisfaction, never, however, allowing their exuberance to degenerate into unseemly roughness.

_____

Queen Victoria inspecting the Queen Victoria, *Hospital Ship of the Mission to Deep Sea Fishermen in Osborne Bay.*

1. Hospital on Board the Queen Victoria. *2. The Surgery. 3. Explaining to the Royal Party the method of Conveying the Sick or Wounded on Board the Hospital Ship.*

A Christmas Ship for Coastguardsmen's Children: Dismantling the Ship of her Toys.

A Magic Lantern Entertainment for Poor and Destitute Children given by the Fulham Liberal Club and Institute.

A new Boy

Food for the Body

The "Exmouth"

Athletics

Singlestick

Grease

The Noble Art

Gun Drill

Life on board H.M

Food for the Mind

The Toilet

MAN WILL DO HIS DUTY

Turn in

Instruction Model

A member of the Band

"Prepare to Ram!"

Training Ship Exmouth.

Our Artist has found among the daily moving crowds of visitors a few subjects for his pencil, which are characteristic of a state of general leisure and decorous relaxation. This is not a time of cheap holiday trips for third-class London passengers and tumultuous rushes to the beach, where countless Toms, Dicks, and Harrys, with their too demonstrative lady companions, make a scene like Hampstead-heath on a Bank Holiday in sight of the heaving billows of the Channel. Most of these figures are those of members of the families who choose a temporary residence, late in autumn, far removed from London fog and drizzle, seeking the prolonged benefit of a comparatively mild atmosphere and some days of unclouded skies. It is pleasant, especially, to watch the children out of doors; the little girl in her goat-carriage, gravely listening to the talk of a boy-lover, in sailor costume, who walks beside her; the other young would-be sailor, who carries a ship of his own to be launched in a pebbly pool on the shore, left by the receding tide; the young couple playing with battle-dores and shuttlecock in Preston Park.

Music is heard on the Parade, where an accomplished family of youthful professionals, with violin and violin-cello, flute and clarionet, and the little one beating a kettledrum, work sweetly together for the pence, and we hope the sixpences, which they have fairly deserved. An old resident, perhaps a native townsman of Brighton, having nothing particular to do, and knowing all the fixtures of the place, contents himself with inspecting the newly-arrived company, while smoking his accustomed morning pipe. Pretty girls, for whose presence we silently return admiring thanks, in all places and at all times, are not absent from the scene at Brighton; but why has one of the prettiest indulged in so odd a fancy in dress as to display flowers on the surface of a fur tippet? Yonder, on a corner seat of the Pier, out of hearing but not out of sight, a young gentleman and a young lady have something to say to each other, which is surely very earnest, and ought not to be called "flirting". We sincerely wish them well, and hope that this means a real attachment, under favourable auspices, which will secure their mutual happiness for life. Is that other young lady who sits discreetly apart, a sister, a cousin, or an intimate friend, knowing the subject of their private conference, and forcing herself to look away, beyond the expanse of waves, at the steamer which is coming up the Channel? She will expect to be told all that "he" said, when the other "she" has

"London-super-Mare," as it has been called, the lively seaside town which stretches what Macaulay has termed "its gay and fantastic front," its esplanades, terraces, squares, and ranges of bright-looking houses far beyond and far up the hill-sides, a length exceeding two miles on the sunny coast of Sussex, centreing in the Old Steyne and the Georgian whim of a Pavilion in the Regency Chinese style, is a jolly place of recreation for people who do not want to be too quiet and retired. There is plenty of light and air and a wide open sea; breezy Downs rising behind the town; sufficient bustle and shopping in the streets; first-class hotels, and means of dining with luxury;

a variety of public amusements, and speedy access to the metropolis, of which Brighton, in spite of fifty miles' distance, may almost be reckoned a marine suburb. It is a winter residence for many families, as well as a summer resort for sea-bathers, affording home conveniences, and easy communication with friends, to those of London connections, and being rather more within easy reach than Hastings and St. Leonards, Eastbourne, or Folkstone. The attractions of Brighton are not to be denied; and the public spirit of its inhabitants has improved its natural advantages with a Pier, an Aquarium, Baths, and other institutions which are justly admired.

Mountaineering in the Tyrol: Turning a Corner.

Open Spaces for London—Scene in the Churchyard of St. John

hurch, Waterloo Road, recently thrown open to the public.

141

MARRIAGE
NO LONGER A LA MODE

Marriage is going out of fashion! This statement has been made by social observers for some years past, with regard to the middle and upper classes. But now the fact has become so certain and so true of all classes as to have actually passed into the region of our national statistics. The annual return of the Registrar-General, just issued, informs us that the marriage rate of London last year was the lowest on record; and not only that, but the three years immediately preceding the last were the next lowest on the list. In short, the number of marriages in proportion to the population in London has steadily declined year by year, ever since 1883.

So far as London is concerned, Queen Elizabeth once issued a proclamation ordering the growth of London to stop. She would have no more houses built, she declared; because the few thousand inhabitants that the metropolis then possessed were as numerous as Her Majesty judged it discreet to allow to be gathered together. But even the mighty Tudor's power could not stay the natural growth of London; and "the wen", as the amiable Carlyle was wont to call the heart of the world, has continued to increase. Now it seems as if the growth is at last to be stopped in an equally natural manner. Let the speculative builder tremble! People are leaving off getting married in London; in thirty years London will be peopled entirely with elderly couples, bachelors and spinsters; and self-contained "flats" of four rooms and a kitchen will be in high demand, while "desirable family residences" will be absolutely worthless.

A writer on the "Position of Women" declares that women now are less useful, and therefore less respected and less loved, than they were in earlier generations. On the other hand, the late Harriet Martineau, in a letter of 1873, expressed her belief that marriages were even then diminishing because women were advancing more rapidly than men, and highly educated women had difficulty in finding men whom they could bring themselves to accept as husbands. The situation is really a serious one, however it may be explained. . . .

AN AMBULANCE CLASS FOR LADIES.

1. *Practical Illustration of Tying Down the Tongue in cases of Drowning. Happy Thought—Good Muzzle.*

2. *Insensibility—"Something about Tying the Tongue? Oh, Here it is:—'If the Smell of the Breath leads you to suppose that the State is caused by Drink'".*

3. *Stretcher Drill: "Ready." Chorus of Females, "Didn't that Dreadful Thing Move?" They let the Patient Fall.*

4. *Dreadful State of the Pupils at Present.*

5. *Reads, "'As it facilitates the lifting of Patient, he is to clasp one or both arms round the neck of No. 1'. Query, What if I be No. 1?"*

The children and their mothers start from the railway station.

Off at last, on the way to the green fields.

Returning in the evening, with spoils, after a pleasant holiday.

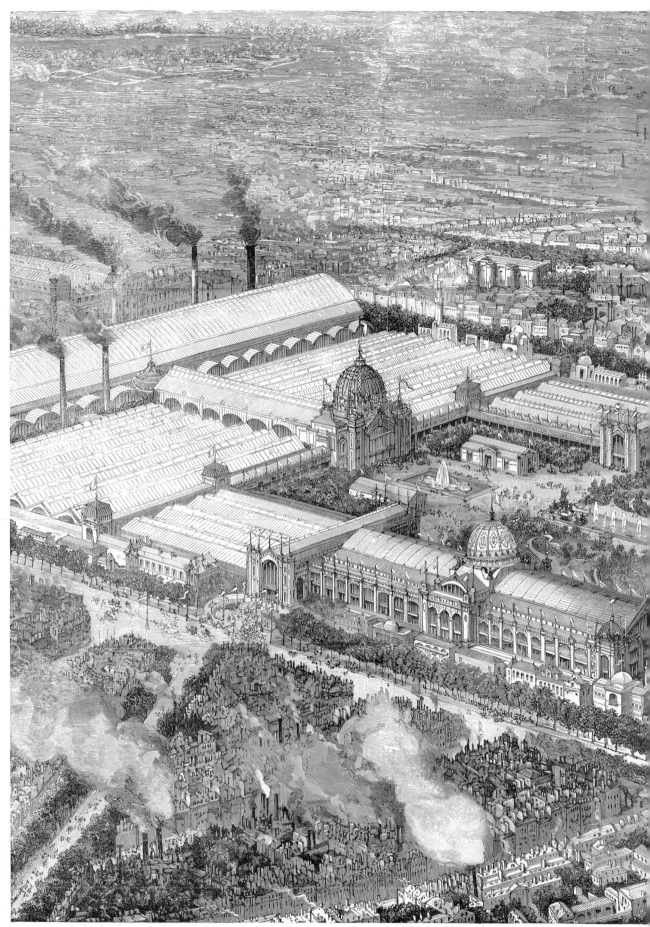

Bird's-eye view of the Paris Exhibitio

uildings and grounds, May 1889.

The Queen and the Bluecoat Boys—Her Majesty inspecting the Christ's Hospital Boys' Drawings in the Picture Gallery, Buckingham Palace.

School Children's Strikes—Juvenile Strikers parading their Grievances.

Passing through a Mangrove Swamp.

Our engraving, which is from a sketch by Mr. F. W. Airey, H.M.S. *Magpie*, represents a shooting-party landed from one of Her Majesty's gunboats on the West Coast of Africa, thirty miles up the river Bonny in quest of game; not for sport exactly, but more for "the pot", to increase their stock of fresh provisions. Having proceeded up the river by canoe as far as the water will allow them, they have disembarked and have landed across the black and nauseous mudbank (over which armies of small crabs and globe-fish disport themselves as cheerily as Thames mudlarks). Arriving on *terra firma*, they follow a narrow track through the thick African bush, until suddenly they burst upon a small native village. They are welcomed by loud, frightened shrieks and yells from the natives, as they, men, women, and children, run from the white men into the bush.

Catching a rheumaticy, fossilised old man, who makes vain attempts to hobble off, they ask him with many promises of "dash" (*i.e.* backsheesh), to show them where to find game, not forgetting the village of the chief they want to find. Having recovered from his fright, the antediluvian copper-coloured old sinner consents, and then commences the "tug of war". For a mile-and-a-half or two miles they travel through thick, sloshy, muddy, fever-stricken mangrove-swamps, carried on the shoulders of the natives forming their canoe's crew—but with no sight of game. Suddenly, through the thick and dark bush, they emerge into the comparatively bright looking village of the longed-for chief, and there they are most kindly and hospitably entertained by him.

IN AN OLD-WORLD PLEASAUNCE

The scent of honeysuckle comes through the open windows; pink blossoms of the Judas-tree are borne through by the breeze; the grey-lichened boughs are swaying and curtsying, rocked to and fro by the wind. Outside, green paths stray through the old garden, bordered by many a rare flower, such as the hearts of our grandmothers loved for their far-famed *pot-pourri*. Delicate lavender bushes, dark-leaved camellia, pink-flowered sweetbriar, perfumed mignonette, elegant tiger-lilies, copper-coloured roses dispute the palm with each other.

By the side of the grass walks, tall iris linger, of every conceivable hue, from white to lavender, orange to golden; such is the tale of June. The grey-lichened walls are wreathed with wisteria, whose purple racemes hang in festoons; scarlet japonica interweaves its blossoms; cream roses nod in the wind. Here and there grow clumps of starry syringa, white-flowered yaccas, red azaleas; the humming of bees and the singing of birds making music in the old garden. Overarching boughs, from time to time, make veritable green arbours; the very artificial ponds of the demesne have in course of time grown "natural". . . .

In old-world times the "Pleasaunce" had a charm all its own. Soon these quaint resting-places will have given way before bricks and mortar: at very rare intervals shall we find the "Pleasaunce".

The Summer Term at Harrow: The Swimming-bath.

From Harrow School in its working aspect at the top of the hill, one naturally runs down to the football field and bathing place known as Ducker. "Er" is the great feature of Harrow slang; there is "speecher", which stands either for Speech Day or for the room; "footer" does duty both for the game and for the ball; "ducker", short for duck puddle; "frowster" for an armchair; in short, any word that by any possibility will bear it has "er" tacked on the end. Football is played in a large field at the foot of the hill adjoining the Park and has recently [1890] been bought by old Harrovians for the school.

Ducker lies just across the road, and therein swimming, diving, and racing of all kinds is practised. Every boy, unless he holds a medical certificate, is compelled to learn to swim, though the distance which qualifies for a pass is not great. On a hot holiday afternoon, boys lounge here for hours, sometimes in the water and sometimes wrapped in their large ducker towels lying on the warm pavement, eating the "tuck" they are careful to provide themselves with. Ducker is a purely artificial piece of water, and has grown, by several enlargements, from a rather muddy pool to its present noble dimensions. Our school songs, which touch on all aspects of Harrow life, a collection the like of which no other school can boast, and of which we have a right to be proud, do not leave Ducker out. It may be poetic license, or perhaps poetical imagination, to call her basin marble, but the poet has truth with him when he says—

> There are bridges and platforms for diving,
> And corners for perching you up
> At ease, while your neighbour is striving
> In vain, for the cup.

THE WRECK OF THE *IREX*

The *Irex* of Greenock, 2248 tons, a three-masted steel ship bound to Rio de Janiero, during a gale in the Channel ran ashore, in Scratchell's Bay at the Needles, Isle of Wight, at ten o'clock on the night of Jan. 25, 1890. The crew, who numbered thirty-four, besides two stowaways, attempted to launch a boat, but without success, and the master and the mate lost their lives. The vessel stuck fast, and the crew took to the rigging, where they had to remain all night, and the greater part of the next day. About midday the vessel was seen and a lifeboat left Totland Bay for the wreck in tow of a steamer. But all endeavours to get to the *Irex* were fruitless, owing to the tremendous sea, and the lifeboat returned. Subsequently, with the aid of the rocket apparatus, a line was fixed on board, and a hawser was passed to the wreck. Fifteen men were by these means landed on the cliff before dark on the Sunday evening; and by midnight all but one were got to shore. One poor fellow had an arm and a leg broken some days before during a heavy gale, and, being so disabled, was washed out of the forecastle and drowned, his shipmates being unable to help him. The ship was distant 450 yards from the top of the cliff.

The wreck of the Irex *at the Needles, Isle of Wight.*

LIFE AMONG THE SANDWICH MEN

In Brewers' Lane, close by Charing Cross, every morning are despatched by Mr. Hunt, the head of the bill-posting firm of that name, the bulk of the sandwich men who advertise the latest novelties in theatres or wardrobes in our streets. All the men sketched by M. Paul Rénouard are well-known sandwich men who have walked between the boards for years.

Mr. Hunt has many curious stories of the men he has employed. Their great temptation is to drink. Half a dozen of them the other day were addressed by what one of them described as "a military gent" who gave them store of good advice and half a crown. With the aid of the coin and a vast amount of cheap beer they promptly got as drunk as they could, and are still grateful to the military man.

During election times they especially enjoyed themselves. A general election is an orgy in which they revel. In London at a Parliamentary election as many as a hundred sandwich men have been employed by each candidate, and there was an instance where each side sedulously sought to make the sandwich men who were proclaiming the virtues of the opposition candidate disgracefully drunk. Both sides succeeded, and 200 drunken sandwich men were on exhibition that day in the constituency to the amusement of the frivolous and the horror of the serious-minded among the lieges. As for Mr. Hunt, he had owlishly-blinking employees applying for their money to him at one and two o'clock the following morning, while many men and many boards were never seen again. The pay

on election days is doubled, and hence if 400 men are required at least 800 can be had. Any day in Brewers' Lane quite double the number of men needed make their appearance, and undergo the experience of aspirants to the Academy walls of either being accepted or rejected. It is a life apart. Most of those who live it have seen better days, and many have flourished among the well-to-do; but, as a rule, they have descended from the lower, middle and the tradesmen's class, and are now working out the punishment of a too great devotion to the bottle.

The Salvation Army, which has a hand in all things, has, of course a hand in the matter of the supply of sandwich men. . . . There was a drizzle of rain, and the lights in the Whitechapel Road, never of the most brilliant sort, were dimmed with the mist. The windows of

the headquarters of the Salvation Army Social Wing were dingy with the damp from the outside, and the smell of cooking from the adjoining shelter seemed more pronounced than usual in the moist, raw air. Close behind my heels as I entered the Inquiry Office came three or four poor fellows, rather footsore, and rather wet as to hats and shoulders and boots. They steamed in the genial warmth, and sat down on the forms along the side of the empty room, waiting patiently, as if sitting was a satisfaction, while I chatted with the captain.

I explained that I wished to know something about the sandwich men and their way of life.

"It is a poor one," he said. "You see these fellows behind you. They have been out all day for us. They are very good specimens of the class we employ in this way. All are steady, reliable men whom we can't find work for otherwise, or who cannot turn their hands to anything else."

"We don't attempt to compete with sandwich agencies with cut prices. It is not in our line; we believe in a living wage, and it is only a living wage with these men, because most of them feed and doss in our shelters. And I'll tell you what, if you wanted 500 sandwich men to be here by eight o'clock to-morrow morning, all ready equipped, we could do it."

"There are so many unemployed, or at least men who have nothing better in view than the money you pay them for parading the streets, that you could get that number in a single night?"

"That is so; things are very bad this winter [1894]. Besides we can make our pick. At Blackfriars, where this is done, we have to select, and we get all sorts and all countries represented there. Do we reject many? Yes, we do; we have to do. It would never do to send out some of the ragged, broken-down men who come to us. We try at least to repair them before we send them out. Suppose an employer wants to send out a lot of men delivering bills. We can't send lame men out, or people who could not get over the ground. That would not be fair to the man who gave us the work. . . . A sad life. Well, it has its uses. The men are earning an honest living or doing a public service. I don't know that it is to be regretted on that ground. The fact that that is the last resort is the thing which is to be regretted about it. It is a hard, inhospitable life; still it is an opportunity. Why one of the men who has charge of these very sandwich men was one of them himself, and has risen from the ranks."

Recruiting the Sandwich Men.

Entering a New World: Jewish Refugees from Russia passing the Statue of Liberty in New York Harbour, 1892.

A Salvation Army Shelter for

...men in Whitechapel, 1892.

THE NEW FORTH BRIDGE

The construction of the great railway bridge to cross the Firth of Forth at Queensferry just beyond Dalmeny Park, where the opposite shores of Fifeshire and Linlithgowshire nearly approach each other, with the rocky islet of Inchgarvie between them, is one of the grandest works of modern engineering. It was designed, for the North British Railway Company, by Sir John Fowler and Mr. Benjamin Baker, and has been four or five years in actual progress. The width of the estuary in this part is reduced by the peninsula of North Queensferry to a mile and a half; and on the south shore, the water shoals rapidly, with a bed of boulder clay and a very deep stratum of mud; but the Fife shore is an almost perpendicular cliff, and the intervening islet is a rock in the centre of the deep channel, with 200 ft. depth of water on each side, and with a strong tide-current sweeping up and down on each side. It was impossible to erect piers anywhere but on this islet; hence the bridge must rest on three main piers, one at South Queensferry, one at Inchgarvie, and one on the Fife shore, besides two supplementary piers which serve to relieve the balance arms of the "cantilever" girders, and to connect the bridge with a long approach viaduct. Each opening of the Forth Bridge is one-third of a mile in clear span; which unprecedented width is spanned by a steel structure made up of two cantilevers or brackets, projecting 675 ft. from the piers, and a central lever connecting the ends of the cantilevers. The cantilevers project about 400 ft. from the piers.

Fife Main Pier under Construction.

Running the First Train over the New Forth Bridge, January 24, 1890.

154

The Queen at the Unveiling of H.R.H. Princess Louise's Statue of Her Majesty in Kensington Gardens, erected as a Jubilee Memorial by the Inhabitants of Kensington, July 1893

The Sims-Edison controllable Torpedo in Movement.

The first public trial in English waters of the Sims-Edison electrical torpedo took place on Monday [February 15, 1892] in Stokes Bay, Portsmouth. The body of the torpedo is in four sections. The foremost one contains the charge; the second carries the cable, which is made with two insulated wires for transmitting the electricity, one carrying the main current to the motor in the third compartment, the other to the electromagnets in the fourth, where they steer the torpedo at the will of the operator. The propeller is a two-bladed screw worked in connection with the motor.

THE LOSS OF H.M.S. *VICTORIA*

Not in conflict, and not in storm, but in one of those collisions, which are leniently called accidental, between the huge, costly, mechanically perfect modern structures of maritime equipment, H.M.S. *Victoria*, the flagship of our Mediterranean Squadron, has been sunk, with the loss of 360 English seamen's lives, including Admiral Sir George Tryon and twenty-one

Last sight of the Stern of the Victoria.

other officers.

On Thursday, June 22 [1893], five miles from Tripoli, on the coast of northern Syria, the Mediterranean Squadron was passing three-quarters of a mile off the shore. The sea was perfectly calm; it was 3.41 in the afternoon. The squadron was formed in two parallel lines, distant the one from the other about six cable lengths, each vessel maintaining a distance of two cable lengths from the next. The *Victoria* led the line nearest the shore, and *Camperdown* leading the corresponding line, composed of the second division under command of Rear-Admiral Albert Hastings Markham. Sir George Tryon gave the order to convert this formation into that of single file. To effect this change each line of vessels had to turn inward upon itself. In executing the manoeuvre, the *Camperdown* collided with the *Victoria*, striking her in the bows. The ram of the former struck the other leading vessel with tremendous force, crashing right into her centre. Then Sir George Tryon turned the *Victoria*'s head towards the land with the object of endeavouring to run her ashore. It was evident that the damage inflicted left no alternative. The water poured in so rapidly that the prow of the *Victoria* soon began to settle down, until she assumed a perpendicular attitude, her stern standing for a few minutes straight up out of the water. She then turned right over and sank ten minutes after the collision.

A VIEW OF
SARAH BERNHARDT

It is one of the penalties of greatness that, at some time or other, a sense of disappointment should steal upon us to destroy the charms of illusion. It cannot be denied that Sarah Bernhardt is not the actress she was. It is not that she has merely lost the grace, the movement, and the willowy elegance of a young woman; it is not merely that the golden tones in her voice have become blurred by incessant travelling and overwork. That the actress is more matronly and less pliable most people will admit. But the actress is not responsible for these things. She alone is not able to stop the hands on Time's dial. But she is a different actress in another respect. Her method is less artistic; and these long tours, this incessant starring have induced a careless and indifferent tone—a scrambling, hurried method of delivery, and evident signs of weariness that are much to be deplored. Even in her best days, at the Théâtre Français, refinement was not

The Victoria capsizing after the collision.

Finishing touches: Madame Sarah Bernhardt in her dressing-room.

one of Sarah Bernhardt's strong points. She was ever inclined to emphasise the shrewish part of a woman's temperament; but the discipline and surroundings of the Comédie-Française held her in some sort of bondage. Left to herself, alone and uninfluenced, she is more inclined to forget the refinement and dignity that are amongst the essentials of her art. It was noticed, in the second act of "La Tosca," the other day [August, 1888], that Sarah Bernhardt adopted an unnecessarily familiar tone, suggesting that the presence of so very ill-bred a person was wholly out of place in a Queen's presence. For this there was no authority in the play. The Tosca was not supposed to be a bad specimen of a public singer, and it is certain that if she did not know how to behave she would not be admitted to the salon of so highly-bred a lady as the Queen of Naples. But, on further study of the art of the actress, it will be observed that the reading of this act—which might have been put down merely

M. Emile Zola reading his paper on "L'Anonymat dans la Presse" at the Conference of the Journalists' Institute in Lincolns Inn Hall.

"I wish to speak of anonymity in journalism. This is a question by which I have been much struck: and if you consider an English newspaper, in which not a single article is signed, and a French newspaper, in which everything is signed you will find yourself, I believe, confronted by the two races, with all that the national temperament, the manners, and the history of the last hundred years have made them."